150 Ideas

for Activities with Senior Adults

Robert L. Sessoms

BROADMAN PRESS
Nashville, Tennessee

Dewey Decimal Classification: 790.19
Subject heading: SENIOR ADULTS—RECREATION

Library of Congress Card Catalog Number: 77-83205
Printed in the United States of America.

To Carolyn, my wife . . .
   Robin, Jami, and Jon
      our children . . .
      and to
   Dr. Agnes Durant Pylant
    Miss Adelle Carlson
      Mrs. Sarah Walton Miller . .
   who inspired me
    and to

The Triple L Club
First Baptist Church
Memphis, Tennessee

The Senior Adults
First Baptist Church
Greensboro, North Carolina

who trained me to work with senior adults.

Introduction

One of my responsibilities with the Church Recreation Department at The Sunday School Board is to work in the area of senior adult recreation. While serving in local churches, the highlights and most memorable times came when I worked with the older adults in those churches. Those experiences, along with hearing people share what their senior adult group does, prompted me to write this idea book.

The book is just that, an idea book. It has 150 ideas for activities with senior adults. Some ideas are explained in a few lines; others take several pages. These ideas were chosen from a list compiled over a period of years from several sources and from suggestions given by leaders of senior adults in local churches who wanted a resource of information at their fingertips. It is by no means exhaustive. Hopefully, it will stimulate your mind to bigger and better ideas. There are suggestions for travel and trip planning, ministry and service ideas, and weekday program suggestions. It is written for you with the desire that it will help you minister to senior adults.

Contents

I. Ideas for Weekday Programs

Idea #1 Weekly/Monthly Meetings

How often should senior adults meet? This is up to each individual group. Weekday activities mean just that—doing things during the week. However, there are several approaches to meeting with senior adults.

Weekly: Meeting one day a week, the same day each week, can be one method. This requires much preparation, detailed planning, and extreme dedication on the part of the senior adult leader. If the leader is a lay volunteer, it might be wise to have assistants who can help with the programs. Even a church staff member might find it difficult to do a weekly program. He, too, might be wise to secure lay volunteer help. Variety in programming is essential in a weekly program.

Twice-a-Month: The group will meet every other week. Scheduling for this might be somewhat easier, but a variety of programming is suggested.

Once-a-Month: Most senior adult groups meet once a month. This does not place an undue hardship on the lay volunteer leader or the paid church staff member who has this responsibility. Several times a year a weekly program may involve a retreat or an extended, week long excursion. Whatever, a variety of programming is suggested in the monthly meetings (see Idea #64).

Idea #2 Craft Program

(For information and suggestions on how to organize a crafts program and for suggested craft ideas and instructions, refer to *Using Craft Activities in the Church*, available at the Baptist Book Store.)

Many, but not all, senior adults enjoy craft activities. This program may be a regular part of a weekday program, a special feature, which on occasion is inserted into the weekly or monthly meeting, a seasonal event, or done separately from, but in addition to, the regular weekly/monthly meeting.

A craft interest survey might be a way to decide what crafts the group is interested in making. Qualified instructors are essential. Inexpensive materials and easy crafts can be a help to the fixed income person. Create crafts which are useful, purposeful, attractive, and which might be given as a gift. Senior adults have enough "trinkets" at home, but suitable crafts can be a way to cut cost for Christmas or other gifts.

Idea #3 Craft/Hobby Fair

Include in a craft/hobby fair a delicious, gourmet luncheon. The crafts fair should have a coordinator. Categories should be established for homemade crafts, stitchery, nature, Christmas, art, and even the hobbies should be categorized collecting, writings, sketches, woodwork, etc. Often hobbies and crafts go hand in hand, and need to be placed in similar categories.

Have the participants pre-register their craft and/or hobby. This will allow the director to determine the categories and arrange the fellowship hall for the exhibits.

Impartial judges might be selected from outside the church and awards presented in a category of various handmade crafts. If this weekday activity is successful, it might remain for all church members to visit on a Wednesday evening or Sunday afternoon.

Idea #4 Cake Baking Contest

For variety of an old idea, have everyone bring a homemade (from scratch) cake. Award ribbons for:

Best Decorated Cake
Best Tasting Cake
Most Unusual Cake
Best Flat Pan Cake
Best All-around Cake (Taste, Decor.)

For fun, get the men of the senior adult group to bake the cakes from scratch. Award ribbons as above, but add—The Worst Cake.

The cakes can be sampled for refreshments, but with all the cakes there will be much cake left over. Take a half-a-cake or slices to shut-ins, nursing homes, or to some firemen in the community.

Idea #5 Camping

Refer to *A Guide to Church Camping,* for the types

of camps which might be held, and to the *Camp Director's Manual* for detailed guidelines in organizing camps, both available at the Baptist Book Store.

There are several types of camping opportunities for senior adults: resident camping, day camping (see Idea #6), and family camping. There are other types of camping experiences (refer to *A Guide to Church Camping*), but only resident and family camping will be discussed briefly here (day camping is discussed in Idea #6).

Resident Camping—This form of camping usually has the following characteristics: a four or five day's stay at a camp facility; a set daily schedule of activities; a Bible study and a formal worship period; a main speaker; a spectator-type participation on the part of the camper. A more centralized approach to camping is probably best for senior adults.

Included in camp features might be this *suggested* schedule of activities:

> 6:00—Coffee pot's abrewing
> 7:00—Breakfast served
> 8:00—Bible study (by the pastor)
> 9:00—Break
> 9:30—Choice of a different conference each day
> > Mission Study
> > Strengthening Prayer Life
> > Dealing with Loneliness
> > How to Make Posters
> > Learn to Write Creatively
> > Let's Make Puppets

(Add your own ideas)
10:30—Prepare for worship
10:45—Worship
11:45—Ready yourself for lunch
12:00—Noon—Food
 1:00—Free to rest, rock, talk
 2:00—Choice of afternoon activities
        Fishing
        Tournaments
        Chess, checkers, table games
        Afternoon hike
        Craft a day
        Shuffleboard
        Tours of the area
 5:00—Free-time
 5:30—Eat dinner or supper or whatever you call
        it
 7:00—Stunt/fun/old movie time
 8:30—Break
 9:00—Campfire or devotional
 9:30—Turn in or stay up

This is only a suggested daily camp schedule. Involve the senior adults in planning camp. It will create more interest. Consider in planning distance to the camp, transportation, the campsite (hilly, woody, rocky, flat), the facilities (indoor or outdoor plumbing, two to a room or are there cabins, bunk beds, food, lighting at night, etc.). See Idea #7 for further guidelines.

Resident camping can be an exciting and meaningful

experience for senior adults if well planned. It can be
the weekly/monthly program feature.

Family Camping—Not all senior adults will be interested in this form of camping nor will many be able to
attend this type of camp due to the expense of equipment.
For those who do have a trailer, camper, mobile vehicle,
or tent, this type of camping might prove to be an exciting
adventure.

In selecting a campground, consider the distance. Most
family-type campouts are usually on a one or two night
basis, returning home Saturday evening in order to attend
the Sunday services at the church.

A loose structured program is planned for family campouts. It should be a time for family relaxation, fellowship
with other senior adults, and plenty of unstructured time.
However, some considerations might be a morning Bible
study, a group hike, a crafts period, fishing, games like
horseshoes, checkers, or Rook, and an evening campfire
with the singing of old hymns (refer to *"The Old Hymns,"*
books and cassette tapes at the Baptist Book Store), and
a testimony or devotional.

Encourage the senior campers to come to the services
on Sundays. Encourage them to investigate "Camper's
on Mission," a joint venture of the Church Recreation
Department of the Sunday School Board and the Home
Mission Board. For information, write to the Church
Recreation Department, Sunday School Board, 127 Ninth
Avenue, North, Nashville, Tennessee, 37234. This too can
be a weekly/monthly program feature.

Idea #6 Day Camping

Consider a program for children, day camping experiences can be adapted for, thus enjoyed by, senior adults. It is a program of camping activities which lasts three to six hours, depending on the schedule, at a site near the church, or at the church, for a period of a few days to an entire week. The evenings are spent at home. The schedule may be in the morning hours (8:00-12:00) or in the late afternoon—early evening (4:00-6:00).

The schedule is the same everyday and could include any or all of the following program features:

> Bible study
> Crafts (nature and other)
> Music
> Worship
> Nature activities (hikes, nature study)
> Trips and tours
> Inactive games
> Rest and relaxation
> Lunch or supper (sack type)
> Breaks

A Guide to Church Camping, Day Camp Counselor's Guide (Indian, Frontier, Forest Ranger series) available at the Baptist Book Store. These day camp materials can be adapted for use with senior adults. For example: The Madison Baptist Association, Huntsville, Alabama, adapted the Indian series for sixty senior adults for a 4:00-6:00 P.M. day camp. It was a huge success. Try day camps for senior adults. Day camping can be the weekly/monthly feature.

Another suggestion to involve senior adults in day camping is to serve as Bible study leaders, nature walk leaders, craft instructors, or to help with refreshments. Consider a day camp mission project with senior adults.

Idea #7 Retreats

Why have a retreat with senior adults? Because retreats offer a unique opportunity for older persons to have an encounter with Christ, a chance to get away in order to recharge one's spiritual battery, to create closer friendships, and to gain inspiration and information.

There are certain factors which must be taken into account when planning a retreat for older persons:

1. *Distance:* Travel time to and from the retreat site is important. A retreat lasts only for one or two days, so travel time needs to be considered as a major factor. Do not travel too many hours, for it takes time away from the retreat.

2. *Site:* The retreat site needs to be fairly level, not rocky, pleasant to the atmosphere of a retreat setting.

3. *Facilities:* Attractive and comfortable facilities, and if possible all people should be under one roof or covered walks. Consider the place before going with your group. Are there stairs to climb? If so, is an elevator available? Are all the rooms ground level? Are the baths private? How many to a room? Are there conference rooms avail-

able? Consider the facilities before you plan.

4. *Food:* Does the retreat site furnish food? Will they handle special diets? Is the cost of food included in the total price? Is the food good? Good, well-prepared food is a must for senior adults.

In organizing a retreat, a steering committee should be appointed. This committee is to decide

1. The purpose of the retreat
2. The theme of the retreat
3. The date of the retreat
4. Where the retreat will be held
5. The cost of the retreat.

The members of the steering committee are to be chairpersons of subcommittees. These committees are made up of two or three other persons. They are:

Program Committee
Publicity Committee
Registration Committee
Recreation Committee
Food Committee (if needed, or in charge of
    refreshments)
Transportation Committee

These persons handle their aspects of the retreat program in cooperation with the retreat director.

For retreat ideas, consult the *Church Recreation Magazine, Mature Living, a Guide to Planning,* and *Conducting A Retreat* (which has a full retreat planned especially for senior adults), the retreat kits *Agape; Koinonia; Prayer, Language of the Spirit;* and *Loneliness.* Check with your

Baptist Book Store and on the Church Literature order
form for the above materials.

A retreat twice a year might be scheduled, but don't
forget to check with your state convention for state-spon-
sored senior adult retreats, the week-long Sunday School
Board—sponsored spring Jubilees at Ridgecrest and the
fall Chautauquas at Ridgecrest and Glorieta Conference
Centers. For information write to Senior Adult Section,
Family Ministry Department, Sunday School Board, 127
Ninth Avenue, North, Nashville, Tennessee, 37234.

Idea #8 Drama

Senior adults and drama go hand in hand. Oftentimes
we do not use senior adults in dramas when the part
calls for a senior adult. We need to incorporate into any
drama the senior adult when a part calls for one.

Drama is a multifaceted program and involves many
forms of dramatic expression:

Monologues

This form of drama requires only one person, speaking alone. For the moment, the speaker becomes another
person and speaks in the first person. He can move freely
about the stage area and involve actions that will get
his point across to the audience. A monologue can be
used in a worship service, during an opening period of
Sunday School or Church Training, at a retreat, at a
fellowship, a campfire, etc.

Storytelling

This is an art form. To be a good storyteller requires imagination and ability to communicate. A good storyteller can paint a picture with words to hold the listener's attention. Storytelling can be used in worship services, in a Sunday School class, at a missions meeting, part of a choir special, at a campfire, etc. Storytelling has great potential for the church and the religious education program. Senior adults are naturals for telling interesting and pointed illustrations by reaching back into experience to illustrate a point.

Pantomime

A pantomime is relating a drama without using words. It is a means of communication through body movements, gestures, and facial expressions to get across a message. It represents a deed, an emotion, an event, or an attitude. Pantomime can be accompanied by music, words, or sound effects to give extra dimensions to communications. A very effective pantomime for senior adults is to work out various movements to a hymn and pantomime it as a choir special. "The Lord's Prayer" or "When I Survey the Wonderous Cross" are two effective sacred numbers that senior adults can place added emphasis through pantomime.

Puppetry

Puppetry can be used in many ways in a church. Refer to the book, *Using Puppetry in the Church* for puppet patterns and ways to make puppets and use puppets in the church. The book, *Puppet Scripts for Use at*

Church, available with a cassette tape of scripts already prepared for use, is also a good resource. There are puppets already prepared and ready for use. There are three families of these puppets, small, medium, and large. The books and puppets are all available at the Baptist Book Store.

Many people enjoy making puppets. Puppets can be constructed from socks, Styrofoam balls, furry materials, boxes, paper plates, and other materials. Puppets can be used to make announcements, tell stories, used at fellowships for a fun drama, and in many other ways. It takes practice to produce puppets correctly, but in the long run this practice pays off with fun and ministry for senior adults.

Role Playing

Role playing can be used in Sunday School, Church Training, at a weekday meeting, on retreats, and many other places. It is simply taking a problem or situation and acting it out. It is unrehearsed and spontaneous. The participants act out situations without a script. Since the situations are only make-believe, the freedom of the participants to experiment and take several approaches involves little risk as it would if the situation were actual and true to life. After the situation has been acted out, the audience or group reacts to what was done.

Tableau

One of the simplest, yet a very effective approach to drama is tableau. It is posing as a picture or a statue. There is no movement on the part of the participant.

He just stands in one place while inspirational music is played or someone reads an inspirational piece. Facial expressions communicate much of what is being translated.

One church used a tableau of the virgin Mary, dressed in white, placed in the baptistery as Christmas music was played. Others have used various characters of the Bible, dressed in costumes standing in the baptistery while a message was preached.

There are many ways to use tableaux, and senior adults can add much to the dramatic effect.

Choral Speaking

Senior adults can be most effective with choral reading. A senior adult speech choir can rehearse and present both humorous and serious pieces to the audience or congregation. Choral speaking is simply trying to communicate a message to the audience. It is a disciplined, rehearsed work which requires timing and vocal inflection. It is as one mighty voice speaking. There are times that many speak, one person might speak, only men, only women, or whatever array of methods one might wish to employ. One effective method of choral speaking is having the Scriptures shared through a choral choir of senior adults during a worship service.

Pageantry

This type of drama is used to celebrate a major event of history. For churches, this means an anniversary celebration. One church celebrated its 125th anniversary with a pageant. Many senior adults portrayed characters of

the past, helped to collect data for the script, wrote much
of the pageant, and served in other areas in the production. It was, more or less, their work and their pageant.
After all, who would know more about the history of
a church than those who helped make it?

Play Production

Most people think this is the only method of drama.
To produce a play takes much work. For helpful guid-
ance, refer to the book, *Introduction to Church Drama.*
Two other books which are also available at the Baptist
Book Store are *Drama in Creative Worship* and *Extra
Dimensions in Church Drama.*

There are many church dramas, one act to three
act plays, available at the Baptist Book Store. There
are even dramas specifically written for senior adults and
even a senior adult musical. Check these resources for
your senior adult group.

A drama presentation of a play might be done for
an evening worship service, an after church fellowship,
a missionary emphasis, or for an opening period at Sunday
School. There are many times to use a play, but rehearsals
are a must for effective results.

Fun Drama

Skits or stunts are what we consider fun drama. It
can be an unrehearsed stunt, one which is read by the
volunteers from the audience, a prepared skit, a group
involvement through a funny reading, or a monologue
type of thing. The best resource for this type of drama
is *Drama for Fun* available at the Baptist Book Store.

These types of dramas can be used at fellowships, camps, retreats, banquets, parties, and picnics. They might be used at some weekday programs, just to break the ice.

Therefore, there is much to drama. Involve your senior adults in this type of activity. From the interest survey you can discover the areas of interests in drama. Include in this the idea of a kazoo band (Idea #11), for there is much drama involved in these productions. Senior adults and drama? They go hand in hand.

Idea #9 Music

Music comes in all forms, but the purpose here is to suggest ways to involve senior adults in music. Almost everyone enjoys singing. For senior adults, the songbook, *Songs to See and Sing* is available at the Baptist Book Store. This large-print edition includes old favorites, fun songs, and spiritual music. It is a good songbook to use for sing-alongs with senior adults at a weekday meeting, at retreats, or while riding the bus on a trip.

Ideas for a weekday program involving music:

Sing-along—Enlist someone who plays the piano, someone who can lead the singing, and an enthusiastic group of senior adults for a fun experience at a sing-along.

Listening to Music—Have those who still have old 78 RPM records bring their collections to just listen to and reminisce. If none are available, some senior adults might still have sheet music of an era of the past. Have a piano available with a pianist who can play for the group. They might enjoy singing as well as listening to the tunes of yesteryear. (See Idea #37)

Musical Group Perform—There may be a group of local musicians in the community or in the church who could perform for the senior adult group. Nearby colleges might have singers or musicians who could provide a program. Classical guitarist, classical pianist, violinist, a chamber group, quartet, chorus, etc., could be enlisted to perform for a program. There might be a fee requested, so be sure to inquire before receiving a commitment.

Involve Your Senior Adults—Form an organized senior adult musical group and have those who can perform for the group do so. Classes in music could be offered in piano, organ, Autoharp, harmonica, guitar, records, etc. with a volunteer instructor in charge.

Many senior adult groups are involved in an organized touring choir (Idea #10), an organized kazoo band (Idea #11), and/or a handbell choir (Idea #12).

Music, whatever the form, is an excellent activity for the senior adult. Have them offer suggestions on what they enjoy.

Idea #10 Senior Adult Choir

Whenever organizing a choir, there are many things to consider:

Who will direct the choir?

Who will be the instrumentalist?

What type of music will be sung?
When and where is the choir to perform?
Should there be an election of choir officers?
How do you plan a choir tour?
These are but a few of the things which need consideration in organizing a choir. For information on organization, write to the Church Music Department, Sunday School Board, 127 Ninth Avenue, North, Nashville, Tennessee, 37234, and request the pamphlet, "How to Begin Adult Choirs." The senior adult choir can perform on a regularly scheduled basis, during senior adult focus week (Idea #134), visit other senior adult groups and perform, etc.

Idea #11 Kazoo Band

Many senior adults enjoy the kazoo band. Some are so organized and talented that they perform for other groups as well as enjoy the fun and pleasure of participating in a kazoo band. Some groups even perform on television, at banquets, at conventions, etc. They have costumes to fit the theme of their performance (show), have soloists, quartets, comedians, and special kazoo numbers. An hour-long program is sometimes given which is first class in performance.

If the senior adults are interested in this type of activity, purchase the various kazoo instruments from a department store (kazoos come in shapes of trombones, trumpets, saxophones, and clarinets). Add cymbals, tambourines, triangles, and rhythm sticks, and you can have a full-fledged band. To get a tune, all the person has to do is to hum the melody of the song into the kazoo instrument. Some groups add a pianist, drummer, guitar, Autoharp, etc.

Select a director, rehearse, and perform for your church at an all church fellowship. It will be fun for both the senior adults and those who listen. For information regarding what one successful kazoo band has done, write to the Ageless Wonders, College Park Baptist Church, Lynchburg, Virginia.

Idea #12 Handbell Choir

Beautiful music adds to a worship service, and handbells offer this type of music. Discover if your group would be interested in performing with handbells. A qualified instructor-director is needed. Of course, the church must own a set of handbells. Music and materials are available from the Baptist Book Store. Contact the Church Music Department, Sunday School Board, 127 Ninth Avenue, North, Nashville, Tennessee, 37234, for more information.

Idea #13 Talent Show

Planning a talent show has some basic principles:

1. Have tryouts and tell the candidates that they must perform the material used in the tryout. Oftentimes, a performer will change his act or add to his act when he stands before an audience.

2. Time each act to see how long it is. Keep account

of the total time the people perform. This will aid in timing the length of your show, and will help in determining the number of acts.

3. Seek a variety of acts. Too many pianos or poetry readings might become somewhat boring to the audience. Also, keep in mind that the talent show is not necessarily a religious service (everyone plays or sings a hymn, gives their testimony, etc.). It is fine to have some religious selections. Have them at the closing of the show in order to end on a devotional note.

The senior adult talent show can be performed at a banquet, weekday meeting (especially if another group is invited for the occasion), a fellowship, or a family night feature.

Idea #14 Parties

One aspect of social recreation is parties. A party is composed of games and refreshments. Most parties have a theme and consist of active and inactive games. Parties last from one to several hours, depending on the group and the occasion.

In planning any party, one might consider the following guidelines:

1. Organize a steering committee composed of chairpersons of various subcommittees. The function of the steering committee is to determine the purpose of the party, choose a theme, decide upon a date and hour for the party, select a place to have the party, and decide for whom the party is planned.

2. The subcommittees will plan the functions they are assigned (these are self-explanatory): publicity, decorations, program (games and other features), refreshments, and cleanup. Each subcommittee can have two or three members to help with the party.

3. The party leader should be aware of certain guidelines as he conducts the party:

(1) Begin and end on time.

(2) Arrange the room before the party.

(3) See that all persons responsible for refreshments, stunts, devotion, etc., are on time and prepared.

(4) Outline the party in detail. On a card write down the schedule. An example:

> Pre-party activity
> Icebreaker
> Mixer
> Game
> Stunt
> Game
> Fun singing
> Game
> Refreshments
> Devotion

(5) Know the rules of the game well enough not to have to refer to them. Stand where everyone can see you. Speak distinctly, but do not strain your voice. Demonstrate the game, be sure everyone understands before playing starts.

(6) End a game at the peak of fun. Do not drag a

game on and on until everyone is totally bored with it. Have enough games so as not to run short. Be over-prepared.

Parties for senior adults can be fun. Note other ideas in this chapter on some parties planned in detail, or refer to *Social Recreation and the Church* and *Senior Adult Mixers* available at the Baptist Book Store. There are many party ideas in the *Church Recreation Magazine, Mature Living,* and other periodicals available through the Church Literature Department. Order from the Sunday School Board, 127 Ninth Avenue, North, Nashville, Tennessee, 37234.

Idea #15 Banquets

A banquet is almost self-explanatory. It is an occasion where people ga er for a formal meal followed by some type of program banquet usually is held for a purpose, or because of a season of the year, or some special celebration. The banquet, like the party, should have a steering committee composed of persons who will serve as heads of subcommittees. The steering committee will decide on such items as:

    Purpose of the banquet
    Theme for the banquet
    Time and place
    Cost and tickets
    Dress—formal or informal

The subcommittees will be chaired by a person and will have several persons serving on the committee (dependent on the size of the banquet as to the size of the subcommittee). Such subcommittees are:

Publicity
Program
Decorations
Food
Tickets and reservations
Reception
Transportation (if needed)

There are several items the banquet leader must consider:

1. Pre-banquet activities: Should hors d'oeuvres be served? What about a mixer to seat people at tables? Are name tags or name cards to be used?

2. Toastmaster: Who will be the toastmaster? Is he to preside over the entire banquet? Where will he sit?

3. Invocation: Who will do it? When will it be said?

4. Welcome: By the banquet chairperson or the toastmaster?

5. Meal: Will music be played during the meal? Is it buffet or do you have servers? Do you gather the dishes before or after the entertainment?

6. Recognitions: Special guests, special awards, committee appreciation, etc.

7. Icebreaker: What about a game at the table? Group singing?

8. Special music: What type of music—sacred or secular; light or heavy?

9. Speaker or special program feature: Will you have

a speaker, a fun drama prepared, a musical group, a comedian, a movie, slides, a serious speaker, the preacher, or what?

10. Benediction: By whom?

With the senior adults all dressed up, have someone take Polaroid photos of them (individually or couples), and give to them as a remembrance.

For banquet ideas, consult the *Church Recreation Magazine, Mature Living, Social Recreation and the Church, Four Seasons Party and Banquet Book*, available at the Baptist Book Store.

Idea #16 Fellowship

The difference between a fellowship and a party is that a fellowship usually follows something and lasts one hour or less. It could be an after church fellowship just for senior adults, a fellowship after a Bible study or a program, or a fellowship at someone's home after a trip.

There are different events which take place during a fellowship. There can be games, fun singing, a fun drama, mental games, entertainment, a film, a speaker, or whatever. Have a variety in fellowship planning. Refreshments are a must at most social gatherings. End a fellowship on a serious note with a devotional. For ideas, check the *Church Recreation Magazine, Mature Living, Social Recreation and the Church, How to Plan and Conduct Fellowship Activities in the Church,* and *Senior Adult Mixers.*

Idea #17 Sports

Just because someone is retired does not necessarily
mean that he has abandoned sports activities. The senior
adult survey (Idea #147) will help in planning sporting
events for this age group. Consider a golf tournament,
a shuffleboard tournament, a fishing rodeo (Idea #26),
sports clinics for this age group, swimming, bowling,
cycling, or horseshoes. There are many sporting events
which senior adults can participate in and enjoy. Consult
*A Guide to Using Sports and Games in the Life of the
Church.*

Idea #18 Tournaments

Checkers, chess, Chinese checkers, dominoes, back-
gammon, Rook, billiards, pool, shuffleboard, and other
types of games can be fun and interesting for senior adults.
Keep a ladder tournament going on some of these. Compete with other churches on a checkers or chess tournament. Horseshoes is an activity that might be fun in
tournament play—singles and doubles. In any case, check
to see if your senior adults might enjoy a tournament
during a month or period of time. For types of tour-
naments, see *A Guide to Using Sports and Games in the
Life of the Church.*

Idea #19 Physical Fitness

To go into any type of requirements, schedules, etc.,
would take a volume. Senior adults, just like anyone else,
need a program of physical fitness. This involves a pro-

gram of walking or jogging and proper nutrition. It requires a complete physical examination by their physician, a program set up by a qualified physical fitness instructor, and a disciplined program which must be followed. Local YMCA personnel or high school/college physical educators might be the persons to help organize and set up such a program for your senior adults.

Idea #20 Everybody's Birthday Party

Many senior adult groups will have a cake at the monthly meeting for those who celebrate a birthday during the month. Some groups might include sending cards on birthdays. But, one of the biggest "goofs" in a senior adult program is to let a month slip by and fail to recognize in any way the birthdays of seniors by having a meeting canceled due to weather. To remedy this possibility, have "Everybody's Birthday Party" during the first month of the year—January—at the first meeting. Have ice cream and cake. Have twelve tables with materials to decorate with (a table for each month), and let everyone decorate the table for their birthday month. Sing happy birthday, and have everyone bring a white elephant gift (see Idea #35) or a small gift so that everyone will receive a birthday present. As in any party, plan games for the group to play.

Idea #21 Golden Wedding Anniversary

This occasion may not be a regular event, but when

a couple arrives at this milestone or other anniversaries which are longer—fifty-five, sixty, or sixty-five years, plan a special recognition. Most of these events are centered around a reception type of event. It is best to work with members of the family so as not to conflict with plans they might have to observe this anniversary. If the family is planning an event, your group might like to hold a special occasion for the couple with a "This Is Your Life" type of program, or display photographs of the couple from their wedding to the present. In any case, special recognition is worthy.

Idea #22 Family Tree

One of the fastest growing hobbies is genealogy, a study of the family tree. Have a meeting and all those who have a family crest bring them to show. Those who have the story on the origin of their name, their genealogy traced as far back as the ancestor who first came to America, facts about a famous relative, and/or so on, each share. Each person (family) is allowed a predetermined amount of time to share. Old photographs or Bibles can add to the drama of learning about one's roots. Who knows what skeleton might show up or maybe people will discover they just might be related—tenth cousin on your great aunt's husband's side of the family.

Idea #23 Masquerade Party

Costumes and all that goes with a masquerade party can make for a fun-filled evening for senior adults. Awards for the best costume, most original costume, best home-made costume, and funniest costume, etc., might be presented. Have someone take photos for a scrapbook of the event. Quiet games and good refreshments can top off a make-believe party, or have a banquet.

Idea #24 Program on the Holy Land

Everyone enjoys showing slides. But, a good program of slides on the Holy Land could enhance a Bible study preparation. To see places that will be studied in a Bible study might be the thing to gain a good attendance for such a study. Or, just to show slides of the places where Jesus lived and walked can be most inspiring. If the group is anticipating the possibility of such a trip, slides might create a more positive response from the group planning to go. In any case, this could be a good program idea, unless the pastor has shown his slides every year.

Idea #25 Trips by Films

When the weather is too cold to go on long trips, or even short trips, trips by films might be just the thing for your group. There are many sources for films and many excellent ones to view. For example: The film about Mount Everest issued by *National Geographic* was shown to a group of senior adults. During the trip by film as the climbers climbed Mount Everest, members of the group kept leaving the room. At the completion of the film, the lights were turned on, and all the group had left the room to get their winter coats. When asked why—they replied that they got cold watching the snow blow as people climbed the mountain.

Some sources for films are:

    Public libraries
    University or college libraries
    Bell Telephone Company
    Insurance companies
    Major oil companies
    Travel agencies
    Military installations
    General Electric
    State Health Services
    Southern Baptist Convention Radio and Television Commission
    P.O. Box 12157
    Fort Worth, Texas 76116

Resources for Christian films and their addresses are:

Ken Anderson Films, P.O. Box 618, Winona Lake, Indiana 46590

Broadman Films—Baptist Book Store Film Center in your area

Concordia Films and Media Products, 8538 Jefferson Street, St. Louis, Missouri 63318

Family Films (Counterpoint Films), 5823 Santa Monica Boulevard, Hollywood, California 90038

Gospel Films (Youth Films, Inc.), Box 455, Muskegon, Michigan 49433

Pyramid Films, Box 1048, Santa Monica, California 90404

Space Age Communications, Box 11008, Dallas, Texas 75223

Idea #26 Fishing Rodeo or Trip

Be sure to publicize this event well in advance. Create interest among the senior adults, and plan for a good turnout. First of all, you need to select a site to go fishing. Most senior adults who fish like to fish from a pier or the bank of a lake, but not from a boat. A date and time for fishing should be set and announced. Prizes for the following might be offered:

The largest fish
The smallest fish
The best dressed fisherman
The fanciest dressed fisherwoman
The most unusual fishing lure
The most fish caught

Add your own. Climax the day with an old-fashioned fish fry (be sure to take along enough fish already caught for this one, just in case).

Idea #27 Picnic and Fly a Kite Day

It is fun to fly a kite. Everyone is to bring along a kite and some string, plus a delicious picnic lunch. Find a nice park with an open field to fly the kites. Of course, a nice, warm windy day is preferred. Award prizes for the kite which is most unusual, which flies the highest, and the one with the longest tail that flies. Kites can be purchased from a store, homemade, or borrowed from grandchildren.

Idea #28 Party for Children's Home

One church has an annual Christmas banquet and party for the Baptist Children's Home nearby. The children are the guests of the senior adults and receive a full turkey dinner, a gift of $3.00 (brand-new one dollar bills), a sack of goodies (donated by others in the church or community) and a program is presented (which includes Santa Claus who gives each child a gift). After the banquet and program, the children go bowling or roller-skating as guests of the church. If a Baptist Children's Home is not nearby, then a group of underprivileged children might be the guests. It makes for a merry Christmas for all.

Idea #29 Cook Breakfast in the Park

A group of senior adults in a coastal community makes this event a regular annual occasion by cooking breakfast on the beach. If no beach is available, then a nice park will do. Bring along a large skillet, the eggs, ham, sausage, or bacon, and all the trimmings and have breakfast in the park. After the hearty meal, have a Bible study or worship time.

Idea #30 Hobo Party

One does not hear about hoboes nowadays, but senior adults remember them. Have a hobo party where everyone dresses as hoboes (blue jeans, overalls, sloppy clothes are worn). A red bandanna tied to the end of a stick was carried by the hobo. So, your group can dress like the hoboes and brings along a can of beans wrapped up in a red bandanna tied to the end of a stick. A large black kettle over an open fire can cook the beans. Be sure to have a large pot of hot coffee to go along with the meal.

Hoboes sat around a fire and related travel adventures. So, with your senior adults, sit around the fire, eat beans, drink coffee, and share travel stories. One church did this and said it was a most enjoyable time.

Idea #31 Kids Party

Try what one church did—have a kids' party. They dressed up like kids (whatever that means), visited a toy store (owned by one of the church members), and played with the toys. The ladies enjoyed making over the dolls while the men worked with the trains, racing cars, and other racing toys. They said they had a very good, fun time—just playing with toys. I'm sure that business was good for the owner and there were many happy grand-children after their grandparents had played with the toys.

Idea #32 Progressive Dinner

Schedule ahead of time the places you plan to go. The progressive dinner can begin with an appetizer at some-one's home, the salad at another home, the main course at a third home, and dessert at a fourth home. Reservations are needed for this type of dinner. For the main course, everyone could furnish a covered dish, but assignments need to be made for this so as to get a balanced meal.

Another suggestion for a progressive dinner is to visit different restaurants or cafeterias for the appetizer, salad, main course, and dessert. Be sure to let the proprietor know ahead of time about this in order for him to be prepared.

Idea #33 Easter Egg Hunt

An annual event in one church is an Easter egg hunt for the senior adults. Eggs and other favors are hidden and the senior adults are to search for them. It is the same as for children, only for senior adults. Asked if they felt foolish, the answer was no—it was fun.

However, maybe your group is not willing to do this, but could color eggs and have a hunt for children in the church or for their own grandchildren.

Idea #34 Christmas Tree

An annual event for this senior adult group is to bring homemade decorations for the tree on display in the church recreation center. A craft class to make homemade decorations might be held to launch the program, but in years to follow more original ornaments can be made and brought from home. Popcorn or cranberries strung on string make for an old-fashioned look. Some have decorated empty egg shells, others have created ornaments out of flash cubes, egg cartons, or old Christmas cards.

Whatever, the tree adds to the meaning of the season as senior adults make their tree uniquely different.

Another idea is to have a chrisman class. Chrisma are Styrofoam ornaments in the shapes of Christian symbols. These ornaments cannot be hung on an artificial tree, but an evergreen. For information on this meaningful ornament, consult the crafts book, *Using Crafts Activities in the Church,* or write to The Chrisman Committee, Church of the Ascension, 314 West Main St., Danville, Virginia, 24541.

Idea #35 White Elephant Party

A white elephant is something of value which you will never use, yet you cannot throw away. It can become a gift for someone else. White elephants can be used for Christmas parties, birthday parties (see Idea #20), or other occasions. There are ways to hand white elephants out:

1. Have everyone place his gift on the table. The group sits in a semicircle and numbers off consecutively. Number 1 goes to the table and chooses any gift, opens it, and sits down. Number 2 follows suit, unless she likes number 1's gift. In that case, number 2 takes number 1's gift. Then number 1 goes back and chooses another gift. This continues until everyone has chosen a gift. A gift may be exchanged only three times, then it is "frozen" and cannot be taken by another person.

2. As each guest arrives, give him a number. Place on that person's gift a different number so he won't

receive his own gift. Everyone sits in a circle. As the
numbers are called out each person chooses the gift that
has his corresponding number on it. This is his gift for
the evening.

3. As the guests arrive, have them place their gifts
on the table. The hostess will tie a string on each gift,
place the gifts back on the table, and cover the gifts
with a sheet. The guests take turns coming to the table,
taking hold of a string, and slowly pulling the gift out
from under the sheet. Then, the guest opens the gift for
the others to see. (See pamphlet *Senior Adult Mixers*,
by Robert Sessoms.)

Idea #36 Luncheon for Retirees

Once a month, the members of one church who are
retired meet for a meal and program. These persons are
usually men and the program deals with various facets
of retirement and other opportunities for service. One
program was on how to raise business. These men enjoy
the fellowship. It may look like an exclusive group, but
these persons feel a kinship and need to be together. It
can be done for ladies, too!

Idea #37 Listen to Music

One church took a survey and discovered that over
half of the senior adults would enjoy just sitting and
listening to music. For a program such as this, have each
person bring their favorite piece of music on a record
or tape. Be sure to have a three speed-record player with
a 45 RPM adapter, and cassette recorder and an eight

track recorder, and a reel to reel recorder. All these might not be available or necessary, but be prepared.

The people can bring old favorites (some might even have some old 78 RPM records), classical, religious, popular, marching, piano, or whatever type of music. Each person has the opportunity to play his piece of music, and if he knows some particulars about the piece, the composer, or the lyric writer, he may share these facts. Make the time enjoyable as well as informative.

A program could be centered around just one type of music: a program of jazz music; a program of classical guitar; music of South America; Negro spirituals; music by Handel; etc. The program could be a special feature where the people come and listen and learn.

Idea #38 Model Latest Fashions

A retired pastor described his new avocation—modeling. Each season of the year when new fashions appear, this senior adult group has a noon luncheon and the program feature is the latest fashions in men's and women's clothing. Not only do the senior adults model the clothes, but they discuss how to purchase quality clothing at a reasonable price, how to look and feel good with clothes, how to select coordinates, and so on. Many model homemade clothing. It is an incentive for the senior adults to continue to dress sharply and look and feel good through their dress.

Idea #39 Swimming Party

A group of senior adults planned a swimming party.

Not everyone came, but those who did enjoyed the relaxation of swimming. There were no crazy diving contests, or swimming under water for distance, but just a chance to enjoy the water and fellowship with other senior adults. Refreshments were served and a pool-side devotion made this a unique program feature.

Idea #40 Starvation Banquet

This banquet was planned just like any other banquet (see Idea #15). Publicity was sent out, tickets were sold at the cost of a regular dinner at the church, the program was planned, the tables decorated, but when everyone arrived, there was no food. The idea was to sacrifice one meal for needy persons. The money which would have been spent on food, went to a cause to feed others. It might be wise to inform everyone beforehand that this is the purpose in order to avoid any misunderstanding.

Idea #41 Spelling Bee

With an apple for the teacher and slate tablets for the students, an old-fashioned spelling bee might be the thing. Check in the public library or ask if anyone has an old spelling book. Get the book, divide the group into two teams, and begin the spelling bee. The winner might receive a ribbon for his efforts.

Idea #42 Hen Party or Stag Party

A meeting for ladies only and one for the men only was planned by one group of senior adults. It gave the groups opportunities to share common problems and interests over a cup of coffee or tea. There are many topics which can be discussed at this type of meeting: For the ladies:

1. Now that he is home, what do I do with him?

2. He doesn't want to take care of himself, what do I do?

3. He won't come with me to our meetings.

4. He wants to go all the time, and I don't.

5. Now that we are together more, we can't seem to find anything we like to do together.

For the men:

1. My friends are leaving me alone.

2. How can I adjust to retirement?

3. I seem to nag my wife.

4. I'm alone—I need incentive!

5. How do we live on my low income?

There are many topics that can be offered for an all ladies and all men meeting. There are books on aging that might be taught; a doctor might come and talk about changes that take place; someone could discuss budgeting on a fixed income. Do not have too many of these kinds of meetings, for the group needs the interrelationships of the other group.

Idea #43 Grandchildren's Day

There are several ways to observe this special day. One is to actually bring all the grandchildren to a picnic and have a program designed for them. A magician, folk singer, or other entertainer may come and perform. Have each grandchild stand and let the grandparent brag on him.

Another way is to just bring photographs of the grand-children. Many grandchildren today do not live near their grandparents—this is sad—but, with photographs, grandma can stand and brag about her grandchildren as she shares photographs with the group.

Idea #44 How to Take a Photograph

With many of the senior adults traveling around our country and abroad, many take along the old camera. So often they miss the most scenic shot or somehow the picture just doesn't look like the scene they thought they had shot. Have someone who is a qualified photographer come and share some techniques of photography. He could relate the types of cameras which are available and the quality of photos they take, hints on angles for shooting, how to get the most out of a scene, the value of slides over against photographs, or vice versa, how to mount photographs, etc. There are many aspects to good photography, and the senior adult amateur can learn to take better photographs with just a few helpful hints from the professional.

Idea #45 Preview Coming Events

At the beginning of the new church year, have a program on previews of coming events. This could be an example of the Christmas crafts to be made, brochures on some of the places the group will visit, information on speakers who will be heard during the year, a movie of a place you plan to visit (such as Williamsburg, Washington, Florida, etc.), or slides of places you'll be seeing. Whatever the method, a preview will create excitement in the minds of the people as they anticipate these coming events. Of course, to do this, a year's calendar must be planned and handed out at the meeting.

Idea #46 Looking Back Party

Similar to the Preview Coming Events (Idea #45), this program deals with those things done during the year. It is a good idea to have someone who is good at photography to go along and take slides and photographs of the events done during the year. In May or September, have a "Looking Back Party." Show slides, movies, photographs of the things the group did, places they traveled to, and crafts they made. The senior adult scrapbook (Idea #111) could be available from years past to review some fun-filled times the group had together.

Idea #47 Send a Tablecloth Message and Table Talk

Two ideas in one can be both enjoyable and meaningful. Plan a covered dish luncheon just for the purpose of eating and a chance to sit and talk—table talk. Many of the senior adults do not live near each other or get to see one another except on Sunday morning. A chance to visit over a delicious lunch might be the thing to do, occasionally. But, what about those friends who could not make this meeting due to illness or another conflict? With a felt-tip pen, and the paper table cover from which you eat, write a note of greeting to those who missed the meeting and to those who are shut-ins. One church does this every time they meet and have a covered dish meal. They tear off part of the table covering, gravy stains and all, and send a greeting to someone of the group who was unable to attend. Then someone will deliver the message to the person the message is written for.

Idea #48 Program on Crime Prevention

There are many older persons who are unsure of going out alone to shop, who are afraid to enter a dark home, who live alone with some uncertainty. A program on crime prevention might be a good program to consider Contact your local law enforcement agency to come and discuss ways to prevent crime. There are films available to be shown on ways to prevent crime.

Some areas to cover are safe locks, lighting, places to store valuables, what to do if an intruder should enter, telephone emergency numbers posted for quick reference, what to do if someone tries to grab a purse, etc.

Item #49 Missionary Program

Many missionary speakers are scheduled during the mission emphasis weeks, but there are occasions that missionaries might be more readily available at other times of the year. Foreign and home missionaries can offer a stimulating program. If a missionary is not available to speak, then study a mission book. There are films about various mission stations available. Check with the Foreign and Home Mission Boards for such films. Remember that the director of associational missions is a missionary and could present a very interesting program on mission work right in your association. Each state has a missions director that might be enlisted to share all the mission work going on in your state. A mission program can be scheduled anytime—and be inspiring.

Idea #50 Bible Study

Bible study is an emphasis senior adults enjoy. It is important to have a good Bible study leader. In some churches a retired pastor might be enlisted to lead at this activity. Some areas to consider for study are:

A survey of the Old Testament

A survey of the New Testament

A study of the Gospels

A study of Revelation

A study in-depth of any book of the Bible

A study of any biblical character

There are excellent guides available at the Baptist Book Store for use in Bible study. Many study course books can be used for this study and credit awarded to those who complete the course. This could tie in with a continuing education class (Idea #132).

Idea #51 Program on Health

Health is a major factor among senior adults. A qualified physician who frequently deals with aged persons could be enlisted to discuss problems of health among the elderly. If one is unavailable, a qualified nurse or health officer could be enlisted.

There is more to health than just physical problems. Mental health is a major factor among older persons. A qualified mental health physician could help here. Mental health might be more important than physical problems.

Nutrition is an important aspect of health and should be discussed thoroughly. Physical fitness is a factor also. (Idea #19). Therefore, a program on health will involve more than just physical ailments—mental, physical, nutrition, and physical fitness are all factors to be discussed.

Idea #52 Social Security Information

Because a person has retired does not mean he is aware of all the benefits of Social Security. It might be wise to have someone, preferably a Christian, who works with the Social Security Department come and talk with the senior adults, be available for questions, etc. Even veterans have benefits that they may be unaware of, so someone from the Veterans Administration could also be on the program. For information write to your local Social Security office.

Idea #53 Medicare Program

With the always changing regulations governing medicare aid and benefits, a program led by a qualified person can be of great assistance to those retired persons needing help. A taped program to be carried to the shut-ins might be a helpful ministry to consider. One might even consider printing changes that occur in medicare in the senior adult newsletter (Idea #149).

Idea #54 Write for Fun and Profit

A class in creative writing might be fun for your group of senior adults. There are opportunities to have materials published by writing articles for various publications at the Sunday School Board. Two such magazines are *Mature Living* and *Church Recreation Magazine*. Often free-lance articles are accepted along with poetry and other creative writings. Contact the editor of either magazine by writing to them at the Sunday School Board, 127 Ninth Avenue, North, Nashville, Tennessee 37234.

Some helpful hints in writing to share with the prospective writers are:

1. Have a topic which you wish to communicate, and know what you want to say. Outline the article and write down your thoughts that you want to elaborate on later. This will help you organize the materials.

2. Be sure you know the basics in grammar and sentence structure. It is important to know grammar and how to express yourself through sentences. Remember unity of thought.

3. Each unit of thought needs to have a topic sentence and the words to follow should support that topic sentence.

4. Write simple, and avoid long, complicated words.

5. Do not be too wordy, but express yourself in concise sentences.

6. Stick to the subject.

7. Make the opening statement of the article capture the reader's attention so that he will want to continue to read.

8. After you have completed the writing, read it, and then rewrite it. Let it set a few nights before you do this, and it will help you see it in a different light.

Idea #55 Book Reviews

There are more and more books being published by Broadman Press that are available in Baptist Book Stores in large, easy to read print. Have someone in your senior adult group read some of these books and give a review of them. This might create an interest in a reading club for your senior adults. Other books might be reviewed also. Consult the *Baptist Book Store Catalog* for the books available.

Idea #56 Second Careers

Retirement for many is a time when they enjoy continuing working, so many begin second careers. A program on the types of jobs which one could pursue might open doors for senior adults who know very little about job opportunities. Many jobs might pay enough to supplement incomes, yet not overextend the amount one is allowed to make under Social Security. Many people do not want a large amount of leisure, but would enjoy being productive at a second career. Some ideas are suggested in Idea #143.

Idea #57 How to Use Audiovisual Aids

A class on ways to make and use audiovisuals can be one way to involve senior adults in the education program of the church. Such items are poster-making, clear cells for overhead projectors, slides, making tape recordings, materials for opaque projectors, plus other visuals for teaching. Consult the book, *How to Make Audiovisuals*, by John Hack, available at the Baptist Book Store.

Idea #58 Making a Will

It is alarming the number of senior adults who do not have a will or the partner of an older American who thinks her mate has a will. Many state laws require a will or the estate may not be given in totality to the survivor. A session of what the laws of your state are concerning estates, property, and wills might open a new light on behalf of senior adults.

A lawyer who deals with estate planning might come and speak to your group. Your state Baptist Foundation has persons who are available to come and discuss this aspect of legal matters. It is vitally important for the survivors to know all the paths that might be taken if a will is not present. Inheritance taxes will also be affected by the lack of a will. Consider this vital aspect for a program for all your senior adults—married, widowed, or single.

Idea #59 Settling an Estate

Akin to the area of having a will, everyone should know what is involved in settling an estate. Some might say they have no estate. This is not true. All of us have an estate. Some estates are larger than others, but there is a process we must follow to settle the estate of someone who is deceased.

Some things to consider in an estate settlement: Who gets what? Who is responsible for the debts that remain? Filing a notice of the deceased in order to protect the widow or widower or children, is a part of settling the estate. What is an executor? Do you need a lawyer or can the survivor settle the estate? How much time is required to settle the estate?

There are many questions that need to be asked and answered. The people should have everything in readiness just in case. The wives need to know where the important papers are located. Social Security benefits play into this settlement. Check Idea #148 for a checklist under the heading "Good Grief" for help in knowing what is expected of the funeral director.

This may not be a most pleasant or fun program, but one which is vital and should be presented. It will be of help to all who come.

Idea #60 Income Tax Preparation

During the early part of a new year plan a program of helping to fill out income tax forms. There are many persons who might pay a substantial amount to have their income tax prepared, but if someone in the church could offer his assistance, it could save some money for those on fixed incomes. Check idea #114 which suggests persons who might help in this program.

Idea #61 Garden Instruction Class

Some basic techniques and helpful hints from a person who has a "green thumb" can be of help to senior adults who might enjoy raising their own vegetables in the summer. Soil preparation, when to plant what, taking care of young plants, what to do if infested with insects, etc., could be discussed.

Some churches have taken property they own, another lot or the back of their present property, and assigned certain amounts of the property to families for gardening. Senior adults could do this and have a nice size garden for the summer.

Other types of instruction can be for flower gardens, houseplants, shrubs and trees. It might be fun and educational to have a nursery worker or farmer come and talk with senior adults about gardening.

Idea #62 Community Issues

A program to discuss various community issues by inviting personalities who are involved in the issues to a meeting with your senior adults could become a very helpful and interesting session. During election time, invite the candidates to speak on their views and have opportunities for questions by your senior adults. Have an editor of the local newspaper come and discuss a controversial editorial. Have members of the city council come and discuss what they are doing about any immoral establishments in your community; have the education people come and discuss busing or the overcrowded conditions of schools. Invite someone from the Humane Society to discuss the animal situation. Have someone from the community health department come and discuss community health problems. Let someone from the election board come and discuss ways your senior adults can help encourage people to vote. There are many community issues which might be considered. Give your older people an opportunity to express issues they would like discussed as you plan.

Idea #63 Program Dealing with Grief

Everyone must deal with death, whether with a mate, a child, a friend, or themselves. We all deal with death. Grief brings about certain characteristics in almost everyone, but everyone does not recognize the symptoms and very few know how to handle grief. A program on dealing with grief deals with things other than death: loneliness, loss of job, loss of mate, loss of family, loss of friends, loss of home, loss of income, loss of health. Dealing with grief is an important aspect to adjustment in the aged and a program might be helpful.

Idea #64 Planning a Year's Calendar

On a retreat, after taking a senior adult interest survey

at a weekly/monthly meeting, get your group together to help plan your calendar. You might run into some difficulty since no two persons can agree on anything. You might have them suggest ideas and you decide the calendar. In any case, in planning a calendar, take into consideration these factors:

1. Plan a balanced program for the year (Idea #146).

2. List those things the survey indicated to be of the most interest to the most people in the group.

3. Remember seasonal events and special features such as church revivals, choir programs, mission emphasis, January Bible Study, etc. Consult the overall church calendar and avoid conflicts. If an event does not involve senior adults, then clear it with the pastor to plan something for the senior adults during that time.

4. Do not plan too many trips, especially those that require travel for two or three days.

5. Spread out trips, retreats, overnight trips, week long trips.

6. Be sure to have the events for the senior adults included in the church calendar.

7. Distribute a year's schedule to each senior adult. This will build anticipation and avoid conflicts in scheduling

II. Ideas for Trips, Travel, Excursions

Idea #65 How to Plan a Trip

Planning a one day trip does not involve too much preparation. Basically, all one needs to consider is the mode of transportation—automobile or bus. If the trip involves a stop for lunch, then a place to eat must be considered. If automobiles are to be used, a word of caution: do not travel in a caravan. Trying to keep together can be the cause of unnecessary accidents and delays. Before departing, make sure each driver knows the directions and has a map of the route to be taken. Decide on a time to arrive at the location. Allow time for those who might arrive a little late due to traffic conditions. Be sure all drivers are properly insured. Passengers who ride in a car should contribute to the gasoline expense, unless this is provided for in the church budget.

When planning an extended trip or tour, one must consider many factors. There are two ways to plan a trip which will entail an overnight stay in a motel, or for a trip which will last a week or more. The first way to plan a trip for an extended period of time is to contact several motel chains and compare the cost for one or two persons per room, check with several bus lines for comparative costs of transportation, and do all the investigating and planning yourself. Or, take an easier method and contact a local, reputable travel agent. If your church does not have a bus and a volunteer driver who can donate a week of his time for a trip, then indicate to the travel agent the needs you have—mode of transportation and type of lodging. Should the trip involve tours, in most cases you will serve as the tour guide and will handle those arrangements.

The question might arise as to who pays the travel agent. Most services offered by a travel agency are without charge to the customer. Travel agents receive a commission paid by the airlines, bus companies, hotels, or motels, and the tour operators who book your reservations. However, some travel agents may charge a nominal fee if he does not receive a commission. In any case, a travel agent can possibly get a better price through his connections than you can arrange yourself.

In planning an excursion that will be a week or longer, there are many questions which should be asked of the travel agent. Here is such a checklist:

What type of accommodations are available? _____Motel? _____Hotel?

Are any meals included in the hotel/motel rates?

Will there be any service charge?

Are all tips included? Baggage handling?

What is included in the sightseeing tours?

How long are the sightseeing tours? All day? Part of the day?

Are there any admission charges on the tour, or is it
  all included in the package price?
What are the cancellation policies?
How soon should I make reservations for a charter
  flight?
If there is a charter flight, how do I meet the require-
  ments to participate with my group?
Should the flight be cancelled, what do I do?
If the trip should include Canada, Mexico, the Ba-
  hamas, etc., do I need a passport, vaccinations, visa?
If in a foreign country, what about currency?
What will the average temperature in that part of the
  country be at this season of the year?
What type of clothing is needed?
If a tour, who is the tour operator? What are his
  benefits?
Be sure to secure a complete itinerary.

Whatever the tour is, or wherever the tour may go, be
sure to find out all the answers you can from the travel
agent *before* departing.

There are additional points of emphasis which you need
to consider as you plan the tour. Your tour group should
know all the answers to the above questions and should
also be given the following list of travel hints:

1. All travel documents should be easily accessible.
These items should be kept with you at all times. When
arriving at a location, all valuables should be placed in
a safe-deposit box while out on a tour. Never leave valuables accessible to possible thieves. Hotels and motels

usually have safe-deposit boxes for rent or available at no charge.

2. Know about the places you are going to visit. Be sure to inform everyone about the places you are going. Write to the chamber of commerce in the city you plan to visit for brochures to distribute to the tour group. If traveling outside the United States, it would be good to know the customs, climate, food, and types of facilities that country offers. If special diets are needed, check with the travel agent to see if these can be provided by the hotel. Be sure to have a doctor, or nurse, on the trip, or know where medical services are available in case of an emergency or illness.

3. When on the tour, if air travel is involved, *be sure to reconfirm* all airline schedules. Be sure there is sufficient time between flights if connections are involved.

4. Document all inconveniences. If anything goes wrong on the tour, write down these inconveniences and report them to your travel agent when you return.

5. Pack properly. Be sure all prescribed medications are carried. Carry along traveler's checks—be sure to carry the receipt for the checks and registration numbers separately from the traveler's checks in case they are misplaced, lost, or stolen. Have a pair of comfortable walking shoes, an extra pair of glasses, if glasses are worn, a travel alarm clock, camera and film, sunglasses, umbrella, and any medications for headaches or motion sickness. If traveling for two days with one night to be spent on the road in a motel, pack a small overnight

case which can be taken from the bus and the larger luggage left on the bus overnight. This will save time and energy. Be sure to mark all luggage with proper identification. For air travel, the name and address should be placed both inside and outside the luggage.

6. Cancel routine services before the trip. Cancel newspaper delivery. Notify the post office when you will return. Stop milk delivery, garbage collection, laundry, etc.

7. Be sure to leave your itinerary and telephone numbers where you can be reached in case of an emergency.

8. In case of a death on the tour, be sure to know what steps to take. It might be a good idea to discuss this possibility with a local funeral director. He can give you expert advice on how to handle this situation if it should ever occur.

Some other ideas in planning an extended trip:

Publicize your tour in a mailout to the senior adults in your church and in other churches.

Send out letters relating the progress of the trip as time draws closer. Include names of persons rooming together, motels/hotels you will be staying in with addresses and telephone numbers, the route you will be taking on the trip, and facts of interest about the places to be visited.

Contact local industries or businesses and relate your purpose, requesting any free items which they use for advertising to give your group. Get a leatherette, zipper bag to place these items in for each person going. Also, include a map, felt-tip pen, paper and pencil games, a copy of *Open Windows* (large print) for a devotional guide, and a card or booklet for them to maintain a record of their expense account.

Prepare a daily newspaper before the trip containing facts pertaining to that particular day. An example: if your group is to visit Washington, D. C., list the places the group will tour that day with suggestions as to what to see, places to take photographs, where you plan to eat, and if the evening is free, with suggestions of what they might do during the evening.

Have a traveling library. Have the church librarian select a variety of books (mystery, devotional, fiction, etc.) and place in a decorated box. The traveling library is available on the bus for check out on the honor system.

While on the bus, incorporate some of the following suggestions:

Rotate seats at every stop. This allows for everyone to sit near the front, in the back, and on both sides of the bus sometime during the trip.

Have a sing-along while traveling down the highway.

On the bus's loudspeaker system, interview the passengers. Attempt to make this humorous.

Have a quiet time for rest, reading, and snoozing.

Play various games. Provide some in the leatherette bag.

Have a prayer time and a devotional time.

Planning a trip for senior adults can be an exciting

thing to do. Be sure to include them in the planning.
They might even like to bring along some homemade
goodies to eat while traveling.

Idea #66 Surprise Trip

In the publicity, advertise that the senior adults will
go on a surprise trip. Curiosity will get to them and they
will respond favorably. An example: A surprise trip was
announced. Everyone was to bring a covered dish for
lunch. That particular morning a rainstorm occurred and
the leader was unsure of the response. Sure enough, a
large group of senior adults weathered the storm for the
surprise trip. Most said they came because they were
curious. The group boarded the bus, with covered dish
in hand, and began the journey. The leader had the group
guessing where they were going. Eventually, the bus
stopped in front of the home of the pastor. The surprise
trip was to have lunch with the pastor, his wife, and
to see their lovely home. Most of the group had never
been in the pastor's home. This, of course, was pre-
arranged with the pastor and his wife. It proved to be a
most enjoyable and memorable occasion. The group fur-
nished the food, the pastor's wife the dishes, and the senior
adult leader washed the dishes.

Another way to use the surprise trip idea is to announce
the surprise trip when you don't have anything planned
for the next senior adult event. It allows time to plan
a trip for the next meeting. But, don't do as one
leader—he announced a surprise trip, showed up for the

meeting, and forgot to make any plans. All the senior adults boarded the bus and the leader asked the group to start guessing where he was taking them. As the group threw out suggestions as to where they were going, the leader listened intently. Someone suggested that a new motel was having a grand opening, and the leader drove the bus to that motel.

Surprise trips can also be a part of an extended tour. While on a trip to Disney World, a surprise trip to the Stephen Foster Memorial added to the excitement; and while on a trip to Atlanta, a surprise trip to Stone Mountain pleased everyone on board. Do not announce the surprise trip until it is time to go to that spot.

Idea #67 Visit Local Industries

Perhaps your locale has furniture companies or headquarters for major industries such as oil, automobile plants, etc. Whatever the local industry, plan a tour for your group. Your group may have to travel a couple of hours to an industry, but it can prove to be an interesting trip. Some places to consider: an interior decorating shop, Holiday Inn City in Memphis, telephone companies, newspaper printing offices, bakeries, craft shops, clothing mills, recording studios, jewelry making companies, artist shops, foundries, etc

Idea #68 Television and Radio Stations

To see a videotape work, to meet an anchor team, to watch a local disc jockey do his program, to see a live show, or to be on one is a unique way to involve senior adults in this media. Arrange the tour beforehand and try to become involved in a local production—even if it is a local bit of information that can be shown on the evening news.

Idea #69 Visit the Zoo

Your group may not be located near a zoo, or are they? Check with the state wildlife commission or its equivalent, to see if there are any zoos within a day's travel for your group. This type of trip should be a spring, summer, or fall trip. When you arrive, give sufficient time for a leisurely stroll through the zoo. A picnic lunch might be fun for this outing.

Idea #70 Trip to Athletic Events

One senior adult fellowship makes it more than an annual event to visit a professional baseball team for home games. Local high school, college, or professional games can be an all-day excursion for your group. Be sure to have tickets reserved prior to the event. Some athletic events give group rates. Check all possible avenues for a fun-filled time at a baseball, hockey, basketball, football game, or other athletic event. (See Idea #131.)

Idea #71 Take a Boat Excursion

In larger cities on a major river, there are usually excursion boats for a few hour's ride up and down the river. Some senior adults might fear water, so, check before planning this event. A meal on the boat might be just the thing.

For an extended cruise to the Bahamas or to Europe, it is best to arrange this through a local travel agent (Idea #65). This type of cruise can be the fulfillment of a lifelong dream. Do not make this just a pleasure trip, involve the senior adults in an in-depth Bible study while sailing. A conference room for this can be arranged.

Idea #72 Take a Train Ride

Once this used to be the mode of long-distance travel. Check to see if there are any trains that still provide a short trip from one town to the next. Some locales have old-fashioned trains in amusement theme parks. In some mountainous areas there are old smokestack, open-car rides to see the autumn leaves.

Idea #73 Visit Local Gardens

The spring of the year provides an array of beauty as the flowers burst forth. Almost everyone loves to see beautiful gardens, and most communities have either city or private owned gardens for viewing. Just taking a bus load of senior adults around the community to visit the azaleas in bloom, or to someone's rose garden can provide a morning of sheer delight. Some may live near national-ly-known gardens and can make a one-day or overnight trip to see Bellingrath Gardens, Callaway Gardens, the gardens in Wilmington, North Carolina, or whatever is near your community. Even trips to greenhouses or a florist outlet can be a trip to consider.

Idea #74 Visit Local Tourist Attractions

In many instances, people who live in tourist communities have probably never bothered to visit their own tourist attractions. Some of these might be antebellum homes, an Indian village, an amusement theme park, a former president's home, a beautiful park, a battlefield, an industry, a special building, an outdoor drama, an old fort, a hall of fame, the home of some famous person, the fair, or a special holiday event related to the local community, such as a pioneer day. Check with the various chamber of commerce organizations in your community and nearby communities for these tourist attractions. This list will offer many unique opportunities.

Idea #75 Tour to See the Autumn Leaves

Depending on your location, a one-or two-day trip to visit the mountains or an area that displays all the beauty of the changing of the leaves will provide an excellent outing for the senior adults. While on one of these excursions, there are side trips which can enhance the experience. Take along some hot coffee or hot chocolate for a rest stop at a scenic roadside park. Also, a picnic lunch will be a welcomed feast as the group gazes out at all the colors. The Family Ministry Department of the Sunday School Board offers senior adult conferences at both Ridgecrest and Glorieta Conference Centers in the fall. Both will offer opportunities to witness the seasonal change in all its splendor.

Idea #76 Go to the Fair

What an eventful time this could be for your senior adults. Many states offer a lifetime pass for persons who are sixty-five and over to attend the state fair. Also, many state and county fairs will sponsor a day just for senior adults.

One senior adult group used the county fair to exhibit some of the crafts they made. The group placed quilts in competition along with favorite recipes for cakes, pies, etc, and won many ribbons which are displayed in their meeting room. This might be an idea—to place on exhibit at the fair some of the items your group might have. In any case, a day at the fair cannot only bring back memories of farm days, but can be enjoyable for all.

Idea #77 Take Your Group Christmas Shopping

Plan a day's trip to a shopping center in your community or shop as a group in your own downtown area. Many senior adults need transportation, and the church could provide this as a ministry as well as a fun trip to do Christmas shopping. Allow enough time for them to shop and eat. If there is a large shopping mall near your community, a trip to it might be a good idea since it is enclosed. It will help keep the senior adults out of any really cold weather.

Idea #78 A Tour of Christmas Decorations

Although this is a nighttime activity, a trip to see

Christmas decorations downtown, in various neighborhoods, and window decorations in various stores can be an enjoyable evening for senior adults. Before going on this trip, go ahead of time to see the decorations in order to be familiar with the route and where the best decorations are located. To climax the evening you might go back to the church for coffee, refreshments, and a devotional.

Idea #79 Visit a Museum

There are large state-owned museums, local community museums, and privately-owned museums. Many universities, colleges and seminaries have small museums in their libraries. Wherever, a visit to the local museum can be very educational. Often, artifacts will bring back memories for this age-group. Of course, whenever your group visits another community, the museum might be a place to see. Some museums house a planetarium in their building. Schedule a stop there for an interesting show. Many plantariums are located on college campuses, and at the Christmas season will feature a show on the star of Bethlehem.

Idea #80 Take Your Group to a Concert

Check your local paper, or the paper of a major city, to find where and when concerts are frequently held. Schedule an overnight trip if necessary to a major city for a symphony concert. Some might be interested in a bluegrass music concert. Other concert suggestions for your group: local high school band concert; organ recitals held at a church or college; a local piano teacher may sponsor a concert and children from your church might be involved; a concert in the park. In any case, a concert will be a good thing for some of your senior adults.

Idea #81 Visit a Country Store and Farm

Many senior adults come from rural backgrounds, but early in life moved to the city to work, and they would enjoy a return trip to a farm. It might be feasible to arrange with the farm owner to have a cow available for these people to try a hand at milking. After the group feeds the chickens, milks the cow, feeds the hogs, and in general visits the farm, have a picnic lunch inviting the farmer and his wife. After the feast, go to visit an old, country, general merchandise store in the community or somewhere nearby. Before the trip, make sure to arrange this with the farmer, and visit the store to see if it is a "genuine country store."

Idea #82 See the Historical Monuments and Markers

Did you ever travel down a highway or road and see a large metal plaque on the side of the road? Did you stop to see what was written on the plaque? This might be a really educational trip for senior adults. Historical monuments and markers can be found in almost every community or within a short distance. Take along senior adults in a group, stop, and let the group get out and read the writings. Some might even know someone whose name is on the marker or monument. Many states have pamphlets in their historical commission which describe these markers. Contact your state agency and see if they have any information available.

Idea #83 Visit Old Cemeteries

Many old cemeteries have famous people buried in them. Many of the old tombstones have interesting information about the person, or a novel epitaph. One might even take along some newsprint or butcher paper, a piece of charcoal or crayon and do some brass rubbings. This is a craft where the paper is laid over the tombstone, and when rubbed with the charcoal or crayon, the engraving on the tombstone will appear. Some old cemeteries have programs about the history of some of the people buried there, others have grottoes to visit, others might have beautiful gardens and monuments to see. In any case, a trip to a cemetery should prove interesting.

Idea #84 Visit Churches in Your Community

Some of your people have lived in the community all their lives and have never visited in other churches in the vicinity. Take a day to visit several of the churches in your community. Visit the Jewish synagogue and have the rabbi explain their worship services, or the Catholic church where the priest can explain their mass, or other denominations to see the church's architecture and learn about their faith.

Idea #85 Visit Old Homes

Many communities have old homes. If these homes are not opened to the public, they still offer an inviting appeal. Contact the present owners or occupants to see if it would be possible to bring your group there for a visit. Most people would enjoy such a visit, especially if the home has some historical value. Other homes are usually available at certain seasons for tours by the public. Many of the old, historical homes in some smaller Southern communities are open for a tour. Check you area for a time for tours.

Idea #86 Attend an Outdoor Drama

This activity might demand an overnight stay, so secure motel reservations and tickets for the performance well in advance. Remind the senior adults that it could be cool if the drama is in a mountainous region. Some places for outdoor dramas are Arkansas, Texas, North Carolina, Virginia, Florida, and other resort areas. Write to various state departments of tourism for brochures on what is available in their state in outdoor dramas.

Idea #87 Visit an Airport

If your community does not offer air travel facilities, then travel one day to a nearby airport. Plan ahead of time to inform the airport personnel of the tour and arrange for the senior adults to at least go on board an aircraft to see it. There are also many other features of airports which might be toured: control tower, observation deck, restaurant, how tickets are made out, and other services rendered by the airport. Whatever the situation, a visit would prove fun and educational for senior adults.

Idea #88 Visit a Convalescent Home

There are many people in convalescent homes who need regular visits. Although this might be considered a ministry activity, visits to these homes can be rewarding for all. Your group might present a program or give a party for the residents of the home. (See idea #11.)

Idea #89 Visit Rescue Missions

More than likely, senior adults do not know all that is involved in a rescue mission ministry. A tour of the facility, and an explanation of the program can enlighten many of your senior adults. From this trip, a ministry service project may be launched.

Idea #90 Tour Mission Fields

There are both home and foreign mission fields which offer interesting tours. Contact the Home Mission Board, Atlanta, Georgia, 30309, or the Foreign Mission Board, Richmond, Virginia, 23230, for information about mission stations. There are local mission fields sponsored by your association or state. It might prove interesting to go to a mission station and have the missionary explain his ministry.

Idea #91 Visit Denominational Headquarters

When touring in certain areas of the United States, plan a tour of your denominational headquarters and agencies. Here is a list of the addresses:

1. The Southern Baptist Convention
   460 James Robertson Parkway
   Nashville, Tennessee 37219
2. The Sunday School Board
   127 Ninth Avenue, North
   Nashville, Tennessee 37234
3. The Historical Commission
   127 Ninth Avenue, North
   Nashville, Tennessee 37234
4. The Christian Life Commission
   460 James Robertson Parkway
   Nashville, Tennessee 37219
5. The Stewardship Commission
   460 James Robertson Parkway
   Nashville, Tennessee 37219
6. Radio and Television Commission
   6350 West Freeway
   Fort Worth, Texas 76116
7. Foreign Mission Board
   3806 Monument Avenue
   Richmond, Virginia 23230
8. Home Mission Board
   1350 Spring Street, NW
   Atlanta, Georgia 30309

   9. Woman's Missionary Union
      600 North 20th Street
      Birmingham, Alabama 35203
  10. Brotherhood Commission
      1548 Poplar Avenue
      Memphis, Tennessee 38104
Visit your local associational office, your state Baptist
building, and a Baptist Book Store. All of these places
welcome you and your senior adults.

Idea #92 Attend Senior Adult Conferences

Most state Baptist conventions sponsor a senior adult
retreat or some sort of meeting. Contact your own state
for the senior adult conferences and schedule these on
your calendar. The senior adult section of the Family
Ministry Department of the Sunday School Board sponsors
various senior adult conferences at both Ridgecrest and
Glorieta Conference Centers. Write to them for details
and dates. Plan to take your group to one of these state
meetings and to one of the nationwide conferences at
Ridgecrest or Glorieta.

Idea #93 Visit Baptist Universities, Colleges,
and Seminaries

Some of the most exciting places to visit are the Baptist
institutions of higher learning. There are Baptist colleges
in all the predominantly Southern Baptist states. It might
prove wise to discuss your trip with the office of public
relations at each school you consider visiting to see if

any special event is occurring during the time of your scheduled visit—a concert, special chapel speaker, a drama, or some other event. Capitalize on finding out and create a more meaningful trip.

Many of the schools will have interesting artifacts housed in libraries or museums. Outstanding faculty who have made significant contributions to Baptist life might be scheduled to meet with your group. In any case, plan well before visiting one of our beautiful campuses.

Idea #94 Visit the Baptist Student Center

If your group is unable to visit a Baptist college or seminary, then go to a major university or college campus and visit the Baptist student center. Let your senior adults attend one of the meetings—or better, let them conduct a worship service at the center. Arrange with the campus Baptist chaplain for this treat. Lunch at the center with the students might be just what the doctor ordered.

Idea #95 Visit Governmental Centers

An overnight trip to your state capital might provide an exciting time for many of your group. Visit the capitol during the time the legislature meets. Many states will recognize your special group attending that meeting. Other things to see in the capital might include: the governor's mansion, the state art center, the state museum, the legislative offices, and the state archives.

An excellent trip to the nation's capital might be the fulfillment of a lifetime dream. There is so much to see in Washington that a week-long trip might be in order. A travel agent can help plan this tour, but be sure to include visits to Arlington Cemetery to see the changing of the guard, the Marine Monument, the National Art Gallery, the Smithsonian Institute, the Wax Museum, a trip to Mount Vernon, and of course, all the obvious attractions—the Lincoln Memorial, the Washington Monument, the White House, the Capitol, the Library of Congress, the Archives, etc. (See Idea #65.)

Other governmental agencies might be included on a tour of the town hall, county seat, a visit to the mayor, attending a session of the city council, and a tour of the jail. Governmental centers offer a wide variety of educational places and things to experience for senior adults.

Idea #96 Visit a Prison

One of the main reasons to visit a prison is to visit the inmates. This might be classified as a ministry project, but one church visits the prison regularly to fulfill a need of lonely inmates. At Christmas they sponsor a Christmas party and see that every prisoner receives a gift.

Idea #97 Visit Retirement Centers

Maybe some of your people are interested in visiting a retirement center. Many states sponsor, through the Baptist program, retirement centers for senior adults. Many of these homes are excellent and offer an exciting mode of retirement. Also, many people have friends at these centers and this would give time for visiting.

Idea #98 Regional Tours

Senior adults enjoy extended tours. Each section of our nation offers a variety of interesting and exciting sightseeing opportunities. Contact state tourism departments for brochures and maps as you plan a trip. They can supply needed information to make your trip more enjoyable. (See Idea #65.)

Idea #99 Exchange Club Visits

This is like any other exchange visit. Your group of senior adults will go visit another senior adult club in another city or state. The host group will furnish a banquet, plan an interesting program or tour, and then the group divides up and stays in the homes of the host members. Later, this group will visit your community and you will provide for them what they have provided for you. If possible, place couples in homes with couples, and singles with singles. They can share common interest in that way. Later, a joint retreat or extended trip by the two groups might be fun.

Idea #100 Tours of Other Countries

Help from a reputable travel agent who has had experience with overseas tours is a must. Let him help you plan your tour. Remember the hints in Idea #65 as you plan. Many senior adults wish to go to the Holy Land or to Hawaii. There are many interesting trips to any country. Remember to include visits with Southern Baptist Missionaries while visiting other countries.

III. Ideas for Service and Ministry

Idea #101 Birthday Cards

Everyone likes to be remembered on his birthday. The leader of the senior adult weekday program should have readily available a complete list of the senior adults in the church. Along with the names, the list should include addresses, telephone numbers, and birth dates. It is not necessary to have the year attached to the birthday, although many senior adults are proud of their years. A filing system by months can be set up, with birthday cards already filled out and ready to be mailed. Arrange the cards in groups according to the month the birthday appears. Then, each week of that month mail out the cards to persons whose birthdays are that week.

In order to save some money, have one of the craft classes, a children's department, or mission organization make the cards. With a paper heavy enough to serve as a card, have the children draw designs and color the cards. Fold the cards and have the children write appropriate Scripture or statements on them. Cards can be made according to the various months or seasons of the year. In any case, this can be a project for someone else in the church. It can be very meaningful to the senior adult who receives a personalized birthday card on that special day.

Idea #102 Telephone Reassurance Program

No matter what size church, this is a ministry that is needed and can be fulfilled if just adopted. This program involves several approaches:

1. Telephone Reassurance for Shut-ins: The active senior adults (or any age group from youth up) are assigned to or voluntarily adopt a shut-in family or individual. The senior adult faithfully telephones the family or individual on a daily basis to see if they are all right, or need anything. In case of no response, they can call a relative or someone who can go by the house to see if the family or individual is all right. A case in point: An elderly widow lived alone. One day she slipped on a carpet, fell, and broke her hip. She was unable to move or crawl to the telephone to ask someone for help. Fortunately, her son came by to visit, eight hours after her fall, and found her on the floor. He summoned help and she recovered. What if that son had not visited his mother that afternoon? A telephone reassurance program might have prevented her from suffering that long.

2. Telephone Reassurance for Senior Adults: All senior adult families and singles will adopt each other and contact one another everyday or even more frequently. This is basically to see if they are all right. Or, some other age-group might adopt this idea for all the senior adults in their church.

One major consideration if this idea is adopted by a church: If a person, either party, is going to the doctor, out for a ride, shopping, or on a weekend visit, that party should inform their adoptive family or friend that they will be out and away from the phone part or all of the day. This is to inform their friend and prevent needless worry in case they should call and get no answer. One might suspect an emergency exists and call for help. It is necessary for each party to know what the other party is doing. One person might telephone in the morning while the other would telephone in the early evening. Communication is vital in a telephone reassurance program.

Idea #103 Adopted Grandparents

In the mobile society of America, children and grandparents are often separated by distance and time. This is a sad commentary about our society. Children miss the privilege and opportunity to be associated with older adults. Older adults, especially grandparents, miss the joy of spoiling their grandchildren. Therefore, couples with children can seek out senior adults who do not have grandchildren living near them, and if compatible, adopt one another. Many married couples also need the wisdom and guidance of the experienced senior adult. Here is a beautiful opportunity to meet a need for both the child, parent, and grandparent.

Some ideas for these adopted families:

Share birthdays with exchange of gifts or cards.

Have family get-togethers at various times—
Christmas by exchanging gifts; Thanksgiving for a meal,
a monthly get-together for dinner or Sunday lunch.

Take a trip or family camp-out together.

Share a vegetable garden in the summer.

There are many things these adopted families can do
and share together. But, if the real grandparents of the
children or the real grandchildren of the grandparents
are visiting, be sure that communication and understanding is there. Hopefully, no jealousy or misinterpretation
should occur. It should be clearly understood by the
children who their real grandparents are and the love
and esteem which is truly theirs must be instilled in the
minds and hearts of the children.

Idea #104 Serving as Volunteer Workers in the Church Office

Many churches are short of help in the office. Pastors
may need a volunteer secretary or he may need help
on the church mailout. A service corps of volunteers
available on call to help in the church office can be an
answer to many a church's dilemma. Here are some
examples of the types of work that can be done by senior
adult volunteers:

Addressing and stamping envelopes.

Folding bulletins.

Filing information such as letters, records, etc.

Preparation of Sunday School records for a new quarter,
other organizational records, and tabulating surveys, re-

ports, and records. Other types of clerical work relating to administrative functions can be a project.

Counting the church offering at the bank.

Telephoning persons when needed.

Compiling and readying visitation cards and records.

Serving as a volunteer receptionist for the church office during certain hours.

If the church has a recreation ministry and a facility which houses a gymnasium, senior adults could serve as receptionist, answer telephone calls, check equipment in and out, etc.

The church has many areas for volunteer clerical work. Typing, filing information, and telephoning are but a part of the work a volunteer can do. The local Baptist association could probably use the same type of volunteer help. Freeing church staff members or associational workers can give these persons a chance to do more ministering instead of being tied to a church or associational office. The task force of senior adult volunteers can enhance the ministry of the church.

Idea #105 Read to the Sightless

In many large cities, and in some cases, small towns, there is a segment of the population which is visually handicapped. These persons who are without sight are unable to read, yet, they need to hear God's Word. Those senior adults who do not have a visual impairment, can volunteer to help read to the sightless at schools for the blind, for students in elementary, high school, or college, and to those at home who need this service. A tape service could also be effective by reading into a tape recorder and having several tapes available for several blind persons at one time. There are many ways in which a church can help the sightless through senior adults.

Contact your local state for services rendered for the sightless. Know the benefits your state provides, so you can give help to the sightless through knowledge gained by the senior adult. Federal programs are available for the sightless. Discover and work with these people as a ministry and service.

Idea #106 Meals-on-Wheels

Should a church decide upon this type of ministry and service, there are many considerations. First, this is a daily program, accomplished five to seven days a week, every week of the year. It is an effort on the part of a church or a group of churches to provide one hot, balanced meal during the midday to senior adults who are shut-in, without means of financial support, and do not have the ability to provide a balanced hot meal for themselves. This service is without cost to that person or persons. This is an item which is included in the church budget and can be sponsored by one of the mission organizations of the church.

Another consideration is preparation. What are the local and state laws governing this type of service by a church? This needs to be checked into before a church undertakes this type of ministry. If the church meets the standards set for this type of project, who will prepare the food—a church cook or the senior adults? What types of food can be served to the host of people in the community? There are a host of questions to be answered before a church becomes involved. Special diets? the food containers? will the food remain hot while being delivered?

Consider the mode of delivery. Will it be done by senior adults or housewives who can donate this time each day? What is the time factor in delivering food to so many homes? Who will coordinate and head up such a project? What if a regular driver fails to appear, or calls in and is not available for that particular day?

Who will receive the food? With so many shut-ins in larger communities, who decides which individuals will receive this service? Is it for church members only? Where do you get a list of needy persons?

Here are a few answers to the many questions about the program of meals-on-wheels:

To discover the information concerning local or state requirements, contact the county health department. You can find out the requirements on this type of program, who can prepare the meals, if they need a health certificate or not, and other vital information concerning the types of foods and the meal containers.

There should be enough volunteers to deliver the food so as not to obligate a person more than one day (delivery) per week. Sometimes there are enough volunteers to utilize a person one day a month. However, there needs to be a backup crew of two or three persons who can be called upon in case someone cannot make his delivery due to illness, car trouble, or being out of town.

Some churches have meals-on-wheels for their shut-ins only. In large communities several churches cooperate across denominational and even faith lines. A large Southern community instituted a cooperative effort—one Presbyterian church offered its kitchen facilities weekly for this project. The Jewish women volunteered to do the cooking. Other churches provided the volunteer personnel for delivery. Senior adults could do any of the work—cook or deliver.

Hopefully, this has been helpful in establishing some idea of what is involved in a meals-on-wheels program. Any size community (church) can sponsor or cooperate in a joint adventure to help furnish one hot, nutritious meal to the less fortunate aged citizens.

Idea #107 Secret Senior Saints

The senior adults in one church decided to do something special with the young people, so they decided upon the idea of having secret senior saints. On a one-to-one ratio, or maybe two-or three-to-one, depending upon the number of senior adults in ratio with the young people, a senior adult secretly adopts a teenager (maybe more than one) for a period of one year. During that year, this secret senior saint did something special for his secret teen. On birthdays, the teenager received a gift or a card signed, "Your Secret Senior Saint." Or, if the youth did something special at church, sang a solo, played the piano,

gave a testimony, or whatever, the secret senior saint
sent a note of appreciation to that youth. All during the
year, the youth received encouraging letters or even notes
of disapproval, if the situation demanded it, from his
secret senior saint.

At the end of the year, the senior adults gave a fellowship or party for all the youth involved in the program.
For name tags, the senior adults wore the name of his
adopted youth. The youth sought out his secret senior
saint by discovering who wore his name tag. This brought
about a keen sense of appreciation on the part of the
youth for the senior adults of that church. From this
experience, the senior adults adopted the program again,
but this time selected different youth. In one church the
youth adopted the senior adults for the next year.

Idea #108 Banquet Servers

Churches often have a Valentine banquet, a Christmas
banquet, a deacon's banquet, a Woman's Missionary
Union banquet, and youth banquets, etc. In one church,
the servers for *all* the banquets at the church were a
group of senior adult volunteers who decided that this
was a way of service to the church. The group selected
someone to serve as captain. Whenever the church hostess, or person in charge of the banquet, needed servers,
he contacted the captain of the servers who in turn
contacted the other servers. The group became quite
professional as waiters and waitresses.

Idea #109 Keepers of the Lawn or Beautification Ministers

This does not mean that the senior adults are to cut the grass, but rather, serve as a beautification task force. Many church lawns are kept up by custodial help or volunteers, but the senior adults see that the lawn is a thing of beauty. With the help of the buildings and grounds committee, they see that flowers, shrubs, and trees are kept current (seasonal), they assist in the landscaping of the church property, keep the weeds from growing, see that unsightly litter is kept from cluttering, and so on.

Another idea for this group is to create a nature trail with identification of all trees, shrubs, and flowers on church property. Do not label the trees with tags held by nails. An attractive wooden sign in front of the tree, shrub, or flower will suffice.

Idea #110 Inventory of the Church

Many churches may discover that they are underinsured. A complete, periodic inventory of the church may be needed, and senior adults can provide this service. An inventory is not an easy task. It involves estimating or getting the actual current value of all the furnishings, (chairs, tables, chalkboards, etc.), equipment (office machinery, kitchen appliances, sound systems, etc.), decor pieces (draperies, rugs, pictures, etc.), and the value of the permanent structure (worship center, educational space, etc.). Inventory means counting and listing all items and their value if they needed to be replaced.

One senior adult in a church took such an inventory and discovered behind a stack of damaged chairs, a large order of uncrated chairs for the Children's Department. They cancelled a current order for additional chairs for the Children's Department. However, the important discovery was the lack of insurance coverage, so they revised the total amount of coverage on all furnishings and buildings.

A plan to involve the senior adults is to select someone to head the inventory search. This person coordinates the inventory by assigning people to survey various departments for the various categories: expendable equipment, permanent equipment, expendable supplies, literature, shelving, etc. With enough senior adults involved, the counting and listing of everything could be done quickly. All lists are turned in and compiled. The value of these items is listed on the sheet, totaled, and the sheet is given to the Insurance Committee of the church to evaluate. What a unique service provided for the church by the senior adults!

Idea #111 Keep a Scrapbook

There are several implications for keeping a scrapbook. The senior adult(s) in charge might do one or all of these suggestions:

1. Keep a scrapbook of the senior adult weekday activities. Photographs, banquet programs, monthly newsletters, and brochures can be a memorable resource

and joy to refer to in later years.

2. Keep a scrapbook for the church. If a Historical Committee is chosen for the church, the senior adult could cooperate and search through old files for historical data and items (pictures, newspaper clippings, minutes, etc.), to place in the scrapbook.

3. Keep a scrapbook on the pastor (or other church staff members) for a gift to be presented on a special anniversary, when retirement comes, or should the pastor (staff member) be led to another field of service, as a going away gift.

Idea #112 Develop a Children's Media Center

The name of a media center for the church library is a relatively new term. A media center houses not only library books, but tapes and other audiovisuals (projectors, screens, tape recorders, etc.). Most media centers have an area for children. But, to decorate and furnish a children's section in the media center, or to move the children's materials to a nearby, unused room, or to relocate the children's section to an area of the children's wing of the educational building might be a project for senior adults under the supervision of the Media Center Director.

If this project is considered, remember that someone must be available to staff this section. Senior adults are a natural for children and can do this project well.

An attractive children's area should be brightly decorated: bright colored walls with picturesque wallpaper or paintings; colorful shelves; pictures hung which will be meaningful and enjoyable for the children; a rug to sit on for storytime; a center for records and tapes; and even a place to show movies, filmstrips, or slides. A learning center might be included in this area.

It is not necessary to have all these items or areas, but do consider a children's media center section as a project for senior adults. More information is available on—media centers by contacting the Church Library Department, Sunday School Board, 127 Ninth Avenue, North, Nashville, Tennessee, 37234.

Idea #113 Minute Meals

So often, senior adults who live alone do not provide for themselves proper nourishment. Minute meals is a process by which a single, senior adult can cook a full-course, balanced meal, place a full serving into a boilable bag, seal the bag, and place it in the freezer. When the person is ready for a good, nourishing meal, remove the boilable bag with food from the freezer, place the bag into an uncovered pan of boiling water (do not thaw), cook for fifteen minutes or more, open, serve, and enjoy a good meal. The person can cook several vegetables to give variety to the meals eaten during the week. The two-member family can do this also.

There are shut-ins and homebound senior adults who cannot fully take care of themselves. If a single senior adult cooks enough food and places the food in boilable bags, this person can share with the homebound senior adult some of the nourishment by delivering weekly several boilable bags to be placed in the freezer of the homebound person. During the week, the homebound person can enjoy a balanced meal. What a wonderful way to share and minister.

These types of boilable bags are available at many leading department stores. Sears carries an appliance used to seal their boilable bags called Meals in a Minute. This appliance creates an airtight, watertight seal. Their boilable bags are called Seal-N-Save. They come in several sizes.

Idea #114 Retire to Action and Handyman Program

Here are several ideas in one. Retire to action means to continue to do tasks which require skills developed in a vocation or vacation (hobby). An example: a community librarian retired only to find it difficult to adjust. She missed working with children. To help alleviate this need, she retired to action by serving as one of the librarians for her church.

Other examples:

A retired accountant (Certified Public Accountant) can help the church with the financial records or other senior adults who need help with income tax.

A retired schoolteacher can help with literacy classes.

A retired lawyer can aid other senior adults on legal matters, especially if a loved one has passed away. What does an executor of an estate do? He could help by being the volunteer executor.

A retired doctor might aid in a health clinic sponsored by the church.

A retired pastor may lead in a continuing education class (see Idea #132 by teaching in-depth Bible study.

A retired college professor may teach others in his field of specialization through continuing education.

The second idea is the handyman program. Persons with special skills or medium skills offer their services to help persons in need. There are senior adults who are unable to do home repairs or cannot afford the cost for this service. A person retired with special skills could offer his services at the cost of materials alone. Persons who have special skills in plumbing, electricity, carpentry, painting, wallpaper hanging, income tax preparation, roof repair, automobile repair (tune the car, rotate the tires, wash the car), etc., could offer these services to those who might need them. Less skilled persons could also help paint, do small repairs, cut the grass, trim the shrubs, clean windows, wash the woodwork, wash clothes, sew, plant, weed gardens, etc. There are countless opportunities to help those physically unable to do this type of thing. Whenever a need is requested, the handyman volunteers are notified and arrangements are made to fulfill the request.

Idea #115 Hospital Volunteer Service

There are needs everywhere. One place of service is the local hospital. There are programs under various names for volunteer workers to render valuable service.

The Red Cross volunteer program (sometimes referred to as Gray Ladies) is not an auxiliary of the hospital, but does have programs for volunteers. Contact your local Red Cross chapter for information on volunteer programs in and out of the hospitals.

Most volunteer programs in hospitals are associated with the hospital as an auxiliary. The auxiliary is an organization of volunteers whose purpose is to raise funds or render services. Fund raising at the hospital is done when the hospital administration and the auxiliary board of governors discover a need that is urgent, but no funds budgeted for that item. All money raised by the auxiliary is used in the hospital for equipment or improvements.

The service aspect of the volunteer program, sometimes under various names, such as Pink Ladies, renders various services for the hospital and patients. Some of these services are:

Deliver patient's mail.

Transport patients while in the hospital—to X ray, to the lab, or just for a ride in the wheelchair.

Be with the patient before surgery—just for comfort and assurance.

Do errands for the nurses (go to the pharmacy, lab, X ray, to get medical records, etc.).

Staff the information desk.

Escort persons who check into the hospital to their rooms, or help visitors find a room.

Stay with the family who has someone in intensive care and act as a liaison person between the nurse and the patient's family.

Work with nurses to keep patient's families informed.

Work in the gift shop, which in many cases helps to raise money for hospital projects. These people also are there to help families and friends select an appropriate gift for a patient.

Offer a service to parents of the newborn by taking photographs of the baby. This service is a cost item in most cases.

There are many needs and places for senior adults to volunteer their services. Senior adults have a special sense of ministry as they serve in various volunteer positions in hospital auxiliaries.

Idea #116 Decorate the Sanctuary

At various seasons of the year, the sanctuary needs decorating. Often, this is the responsibility of a designated committee within the church. However, this could be a project for the senior adult ministry. Cooperation and communication is essential in this shared responsibility.

Decorations are usually needed at Christmas, Easter, July 4th, Flag Day, Mother's Day, and for special observances. The regular Sunday services are enhanced by flowers or displays in keeping with the seasons or occasions of the year. An idea for senior adult involvement is to let them be responsible for these aspects of church life.

Idea #117 Community Service

Look around—there are places looking for volunteer

workers. Here are a few in your community that might need periodic help:

Hospital Volunteers (see Idea #115)

Voter registration or election workers

Census surveys

Dog inoculations

Help in clinics during a health drive

Prepare bandages for Red Cross or hospitals

Assist in physical therapy for accident, stroke, and cerebral palsy victims.

Help educate retarded children

(See Idea #105)

Idea #118 Lord's House Committee

Every Monday morning, a group of faithful senior adults journey to the church early, before the regular weekday ministry begins, to make the sanctuary ready for the next Sunday's worship service. This Lord's house committee is a nonelected, strictly volunteer group who performs an important service to the church. They remove all leftover bulletins from hymnals and pews, place all hymnals and Bibles properly in place and in order in the hymn racks, collect all the glasses from the Lord's Supper observance, and remove the flowers, divide them up to be distributed to homes of shut-ins or to hospital patients. They make sure everything is shined, dusted, and straightened. This is rendered with deep love and dedication.

Idea #119 Scholarship Fund

This suggestion may not be limited to just senior adults,

but senior adults can initiate the idea. There are times when young people who have surrendered their lives to full-time church-related vocations need financial assistance in college. Being set apart for the gospel ministry is very special. A scholarship fund for such persons can be initiated by the senior adults and administered by a committee of senior adults.

Whenever a young person going into full-time Christian service needs financial aid, he may make application for funds. The scholarship offered might be very minimal in monetary value, but every dollar counts. The funds might pay for the cost of books and materials only, but that helps.

Most scholarship funds require repayment at no interest, or little interest if the person does not complete his training or does not enter into full-time Christian service. Many of these loans are repayable over a period of five to ten years through installments. However, should the person complete his education and enter into the ministry, he is not obligated to repay the scholarship.

A lawyer might be needed to draw up the specifications and/or legality of this idea. There should be definite criteria included in the scholarship contract identifying what constitutes full-time Christian service. Examples of this type of calling: pastors, ministers of education, youth, music, recreation; associate pastors; children's directors; church business administrators; day-care workers; missionaries (home or foreign); kindergarten directors for a church; church librarians; directors of associational missions; denominational workers. There are many vocations within the framework of full-time Christian service. This needs full clarification in the scholarship agreement.

Idea #120 Pictures for Posters

Posters for publicity are always needed at the church. To make attractive, eye-catching posters, colorful pictures can be an asset. Take a weekday meeting with senior adults and cut out attractive, interesting pictures and words from magazines. Have a magazine collection month. Church members can donate old magazines to the project. With good scissors, plenty of folders or large envelopes, and trash containers, let the senior adults cut out pictures and words. Place all the pictures that correspond to various areas in folders and mark accordingly. Do the same for words that go together—especially the same type of printing. These can be placed on file in a central location (media center, church office, craft room), for easy access to anyone who needs to make a poster.

Idea #121 Poster Making/Displays

Following up Idea #120, senior adults can make posters for the church. Have the pastor or another staff member list some of the major events for the coming year (revivals, all church fellowships, dramas, Doctrinal Emphasis Week, Race Relations Sunday, Youth Week, Senior Adult Focus Week [Idea #77], Home or Foreign Missions Week, January Bible Study, etc.). Divide the emphasis (weeks) among the senior adults present and with the needed materials (poster board, colored felt-tip markers, glue, good scissors, and all those pictures and words on file [see Idea #120]), publicity for the year can be made ready and stored until proper time to place on the bulletin boards.

Displays can be most effective in the promotion of an idea or a week of special emphasis. Tables set in foyers or large halls can enhance a week of emphasis. Items from foreign countries can make a missions exhibit more realistic; books and filmstrips on display can magnify a library emphasis; photographs and a slide presentation can encourage interest in a building program emphasis. Many areas of emphasis can be magnified through attractive and meaningful displays. These can be arranged and supervised by senior adults.

Idea #122 Answering Service

Not to be confused with a telephone reassurance program (Idea #102), an answering service provides needed transportation and/or delivery for senior adults. Many senior adults cannot drive or do not have an automobile. Bus service may not be convenient and taxi fares may be too high for fixed income persons. Therefore, an answering service is a way to help these people. A list of senior adults and other church members who can provide transportation and are available to provide this service, when arrangements are made ahead of time, could be made available to senior adults needing this service.

Should a senior adult need transportation to a doctor, he can call the designated number and set up a time to be picked up. The church office might provide the initial contact and each day a senior adult can call the church to see if there were any callers requesting the service. If so, this senior adult could make the necessary arrangements for the caller to be picked up.

The service could provide contact not only for transportation to and from places or events, but if a senior adult needed help of any type, it would serve this function as well (see Idea #114—Handyman). A word of caution: there should be designated places and events for this service, otherwise it could create problems. Places that are necessary for transportation needs are: grocery shopping, other types of shopping, a trip to the doctor or dentist, a visit to the cemetery might be a real need if a loved one has recently passed away, a trip to the beauty parlor or barbershop, a trip to the drugstore if delivery is unavailable, to the church on Sunday or for weekday activities, a visit to hospitals or nursing homes to visit a mate, relative, or close friend. Your group of volunteer drivers needs to decide what services can be given. Service should be available should an emergency occur.

Idea #123 Sew Costumes for Drama

Many costume closets are crying for more costumes. Drama is an excellent activity for a church, but the lack of biblical costumes often hinders the drama program. Scrap cloth, old sheets, and remnants can be used to make attractive and useful biblical costumes. Gather needed materials, thread, patterns, and sewing machines and have a fun-filled, productive day in refurbishing the costume closet.

Idea #124 Raise Flowers for Others

Gardening may be a hobby for some senior adults. Raising flowers can be very enjoyable, but to share these beauties of nature can add much to that enjoyment. Raise flowers for others (cut or potted). Flowers for friends, shut-ins, homebounds, persons in the hospitals, nursing homes, for the church sanctuary, to brighten the church office, are but a few suggestions for raising flowers for others. (See Idea #129 for another idea with flowers.)

Idea #125 Find a Home for a Foreign Student

Our country is fortunate to have many students in high school, college, and graduate schools from countries other than our own. Finding a home for these students does not necessarily mean a place to live while attending school, although this could be done. It means that some home would adopt one student or more and have the home open to this person whenever he wants to come over. Senior adults could take this activity over and discover available homes, or provide such a place themselves. As an added incentive, missionaries in other lands indicate this type of service is most beneficial to their work—it helps in relationships later on the mission field.

Idea #126 Feed Birds in the Winter

This seems like a trivial project, but one senior adult group in a church has adopted the idea to provide food and shelter for birds during the winter months. Whether done on an individual basis at one's home or at the church, it is a pleasure to watch the multi-variety and colors of birds come to feed. The cost of seed is not too extravagant, and the joy is fulfilling.

Idea #127 Make a Puzzle

With the skilled hands of craftsmen, senior adults can join together to make puzzles for preschool children. On 1/8 inch cardboard or wood, glue and shellac a colorful picture. With a jigsaw or coping saw, cut the cardboard or wood and picture into large, odd shapes. This provides a novel project for the senior adult and fun for the preschooler. Pictures of animals, buses, trains, biblical characters, etc., can serve as puzzles.

Idea #128 Sponsor a Back-to-School Party

For children in grades one—six, plan a Back-to-school Party. A hot dog cookout with some fun games can make this an exciting time for the children. It might be wise to have two socials—one for grades one—three, and one for grades four—six.

Relay games might prove exciting. But, be sure the teams are evenly divided, with an equal balance of boys and girls, and equal distribution between grades. Some

relays could be:
  Three-legged race
  Wheelbarrow race
  Fifty-yard dash
  Tug-of-war
  Hop, skip, and jump for distance
  Softball throw for distance
  Bean bag on head relay
  Egg or water-balloon toss

For suggestions for games (field day events) refer to the book: *A Guide to Using Sports and Games in the Life of the Church*, available at the Baptist Book Store. Let the children compete in a softball game or play roll-a-bat.

Other ideas would be to let the children play favorite games like Red Rover; Duck, Duck Goose; Steal the Bacon; Red Light; Mother May I; Kick the Can; Kickball; Drop the Handkerchief, or some they might suggest. In any case, a back-to-school party for the children could prove fun for all.

Idea #129 Plant Exchange

An idea shared by a senior adult group who enjoys green thumb activities, is to grow plants and exchange occasionally with senior adults in the group. This offers one an opportunity to view a variety of plants during the year, and teaches ways to care for various plants.

Idea #130 Camp Grandparents

There are several suggestions for this idea:

1. Whenever there is a resident camp program where adults are needed as counselors or workers (instructors) and small children are involved, a senior adult can serve as the camp grandma/grandpa for these small children. It relieves the parent to devote fulltime to his task at camp.

2. Whenever the church has a family camp-out over a weekend, a camp grandparent can take care of the preschoolers while the children are in a day camp and the youth and adults are in a Bible study.

3. While the parents are involved in a day camp, a senior adult could take care of the preschoolers during the daylight hours.

There are other ways to serve, but a camp grandparent might prove to be fun, and a real blessing for the child.

Idea #131 Church Sports Boosters

Organize a church sports boosters club for senior adults. Have the senior adults come out in force for the children's and youth sports teams. Attend the baseball, softball, and basketball games of the church. Buy buttons that support the church team; attend the sports banquets; cheer for the team.

Since there might be many teams, divide the senior adults so they support different teams instead of only one team. This interest and support can boost the morale of your church sports program.

Idea #132 Continuing Education

A program of continuing education for senior adults

is involving them in a regularly scheduled classroom situation where a variety of subjects are offered. This does not necessarily mean an everyday occurrence, but a weekly program in addition to another day of activity. The continuing education program can be scheduled for a month or quarter. It does not necessarily have to last for a long period of time. If a program such as this is begun, be sure to enlist qualified instructors. These people may be right in the church, or could be enlisted for a fee. Many retired persons may qualify (Idea #114) to instruct in the continuing education classes.

Some suggested areas of study might include:

The Bible: A survey of the Old Testament and/or the New Testament, an in-depth study of a particular book of the Bible, or a study of a passage of Scripture from all aspects of interpretation could be ways to study the Bible.

Doctrine: The study of various doctrines of the Baptist faith could be a source for the continuing education class.

Witnessing Techniques: A program to train senior adults on how to witness to other senior adults who are unsaved.

Church History: A survey of the history of the Christian church from the beginning, and especially Baptist history, could prove interesting and helpful.

Budgeting: How to live on a fixed income.

Small appliance repair: How to fix the toaster, iron, mixer, etc.

Basic electricity: What to do if a light plug wears out or needs repair.

Basic Plumbing: What to do if a sink should stop up.

Crafts: (Idea #28)

Art Classes: Instruction in pen and ink, pastels, watercolors, and oils could be a continuing education program.

Nutrition and Physical Fitness (Idea #19): A qualified person needs to be the instructor for these vital aspects of life.

Check with the local board of education for classes offered for adult education. Some states offer college level courses free, or at a reduced rate. There are opportunities available, or can be made available, if interest is shown on the part of senior adults.

Idea #133 Senior Adult Vacation Bible School

Contact the Sunday School Department, Sunday School Board, 127 Ninth Avenue, North, Nashville, Tennessee, 37234, for information concerning Vacation Bible School for the senior adult. The sessions can be held in conjunction with the regularly scheduled Vacation Bible School.

Idea #134 Senior Adult Focus Week

Just as Youth Week is held in the church, do the same

for the senior adults. May is Senior Adult Month. A week
or a month of emphasis, focusing attention on this age
group, can be a project for the church.

Some suggestions for a senior adult emphasis:

A senior adult choir can sing on Senior Adult Sunday.

Senior adults can usher.

Senior adults can take up the offering.

Senior adults can lead in worship by praying and
reading the Scripture at the worship service.

Senior adults can be in charge of prayer meeting
(consider presenting a senior adult drama).

Senior adults can present a musical or concert for
the evening service.

Senior adults can give testimonies in every department.

Senior adults can sponsor an all-church fellowship.

Have a Senior Adult Week Banquet.

Have a Senior Adult Week Planning Retreat.

Making it known that your church has an emphasis
on senior adult work can be magnified through a Senior
Adult Focus Week.

Idea #135 Eating with a Shut-in

One of the complaints of a person who receives a
meal-on-wheels (Idea #106), or who receives meals delivered by a relative or friend (Idea #113), is that no
one ever stays to share moments over the meal. The meal
is greatly appreciated and needed, but to remain and
share the meal with conversation can serve as a fulfilled

ministry.

If your group is involved in delivering meals, have the people choose someone to visit each trip. That meal can be delivered last and allow time for visiting. Loneliness is a hard emotion, but a few moments a day/week can ease the pain. What an important ministry.

Idea #136 Telephone Prayer Chain

There are many occasions which call for prayer. A volunteer prayer chain can be formed by those senior adults who do not mind being called upon and who wish to share in prayer for those in need.

A telephone chairperson can be contacted and the request relayed. The chairperson contacts group chairpersons who in turn make calls to several others and so down the line until all those who signed up are contacted and the request is known. This ministry can be most effective.

Idea #137 Cassette Tape Ministry

One of the most exciting and worthy ministries is the cassette tape ministry. It is one thing to deliver to shut-ins various tapes with cassette recorders, but to actually be involved in this ministry through the production can be most rewarding and enjoyable.

First, this type of endeavor should be cleared and supported by the pastor, other church staff members, and your church media center staff. It might be an item for the church budget, but some churches have established this program on voluntary contributions. The tapes, recorders, and duplicating equipment have been purchased by the committee or cassette staff from these contributions. A room in the church, preferably near the media center, has been prepared for this type of work.

Second, a trained media center staff of volunteer workers, hopefully including senior adults, can staff this department. They will be responsible for getting the original tape of the speaker, music, or event. It is their responsibility to set up the equipment, tape the event, and duplicate the program so that others might hear it.

Tapes can be made of the pastor's sermons, music from choir concerts, tapings of choir rehearsals for shut-ins to listen to, instrumental pieces which can be arranged with the church pianist and/or organist, special devotionals for shut-ins, banquet speakers, revivals, a concert by a soloist, a Bible lesson taught, a study course lesson, etc. There are many ways to use tapes for shut-ins to hear.

To organize this ministry, contact the Church Library Department, Sunday School Board, 127 Ninth Avenue, North, Nashville, Tennessee, 37234. Here are a few suggestions:

1. This program is sponsored by the media center staff. Senior adults can be members of the committee, and work on this type of ministry.

2. One person who is on the media center staff serves as the director of this ministry in order to give guidance and oversee the total scope of this project.

3. Have financial resources available to purchase

needed tapes and equipment.

4. Have a good selection of tapes on hand before you begin distributing them around the church and community.

5. Set up a filing system to catalog the tapes.

6. If mailing tapes is one way to handle the outflow, secure padded envelopes with return address forms included. Postage needs could be budgeted in the overall cassette budget. There is a special educational postage rate.

Some suggested equipment for establishing a tape ministry:

1. Purchase quality name brand cassette recorders.

2. Purchase quality tapes.

3. An excellent, high-speed, quality duplicator is Pentagon duplicating equipment. This equipment can do both reel to reel and cassette masters.

4. Store tapes in "Scotch" boxes which have been stacked and cemented together.

5. If possible, have someone on your cassette staff who is a professional engineer.

This type of ministry can serve several purposes: It involves senior adults in a meaningful ministry; it provides services to shut-ins who cannot be at the services or special meetings; it can serve as a ministry to other churches; it can help the homebound ministry. What your group does with a cassette tape ministry is up to you. One of the best tape ministries can be found at the Immanuel Baptist Church, Little Rock, Arkansas. However, you can contact the Church Library Department and order their *Media* magazine for other helpful suggestions.

Idea #138 Choir Mission Tour

Many youth choirs go on tour to perform in a different church each evening. A senior adult choir could do the same thing and inspire the senior adults in the host church to become more involved in their senior adult program. It will also inspire the other members of that church.

Many youth choirs go on mission tours not only to sing in churches as they travel, but go to one destination for a week to hold Vacation Bible Schools, Backyard Bible Clubs, day camps, take censuses, and hold revivals in the evening. Senior adults could do the same.

For mission opportunities contact the Special Ministries Department, Home Mission Board, 1350 Spring Street, NW, Atlanta, Georgia, 30309.

Idea #139 Prayer Group

Ever wonder what to do with that hour between Wednesday evening dinner and prayer meeting? One senior adult group formed a prayer group that met during this time to pray for specific requests. The church knew of this group and channeled many requests to them. The pastor stated that his Wednesday evenings were full of power and his entire ministry was affected by this group of praying senior adults. Fill the hour with a senior adult prayer group.

Idea #140 Disciples Now

Visitation is a good ministry. Many people visit by twos, but one church sends all their senior adults to visit the same homebound person at one time. Imagine thirty senior adults instead of two. This group sings, has a devotional time or Bible study, prays, and just visits the homebound person for a longer than average visit. Many share favorite cookies or cakes during the visit. Tapes and recordings of the pastor's message and of music are left at the home for the person to enjoy (Item #137). These disciples are ministering.

Another type of visitation program of discipling is to train senior adults in how to witness to other senior adults. This group can visit senior adults who do not know the joy of the Savior's love. More discipling, now!

Idea #141 Check-Out Service

A check-out service involves the availability of various types of equipment for those who might need it, but cannot afford it. Such items as:

hospital beds
wheelchairs
crutches
bedpans
walkers
walking canes
television sets
radios
cassettes for tapes (Item #137)

A system must be organized. It should be decided if the service is for church members only or as a service to the community. The service can be most helpful to those who need it. Donations of such equipment might be more readily available than one realizes if it is advertised as a ministry. Clear and concise information can be available through a brochure to the membership of this program. A place to store the items will be needed as well as available volunteers to help deliver the larger pieces.

Idea #142 Senior Adult Daycare Program

There is a need for clarification to be made on the term daycare. Studies have shown that there are a variety of programs which exist under the daycare heading. Before a church ventures into a daycare program for senior adults, the type of care provided for senior adults should be clearly and distinctly defined.

One type of daycare program functions as a day hospital. Services are provided for ambulatory patients who do not require twenty-four hour attention, health maintenance, and restoration, various types of therapy, and psychiatric care. Included in this type of daycare program is the socialization of the senior adult patient to help overcome isolation which usually accompanies illness. This type of daycare center operates on a professional and legal level as a hospital, but does not offer overnight patient care. The services offered, however, are more intense than those of an outpatient clinic. In essence, it is a day hospital with facilities and equipment to offer the best of care on an eight-ten hour per day basis.

A second type of daycare program offers little in the way of physical health care and maintenance, but does much toward mental health. In most instances, the facilities are designed to meet more of the social needs of the senior adult. Programs designed to include nutrition, counseling services, some health care, and recreation (arts, crafts, drama, music, parties, banquets, games, etc.).

Daycare programs can vary according to the purpose and goals set by the sponsoring agency. Staffing such a program requires professional qualifications for the director and skilled personnel in program areas. Comfortable and attractive decor is a plus factor in this daycare setting. Proper care should be given when planning this type of setting and program.

Idea #143 Employment and Volunteer Programs

Many senior adults have many years of fruitful service. There are various organizations through which volunteer services and/or associate work for pay is available to qualified persons. Here is a list of opportunities with a brief description of each program.

1. *Southern Baptist Foreign Mission Board:*

There are programs for persons who qualify and are sixty years or younger. The associate missionary program is available for these persons.

There are two programs which are directly related to the retired, skilled person: The Volunteer Program and the Special Project Program.

The Volunteer Program is directed to the retired lay-man who can serve one year on the mission field. This person is to be self-supporting while on the field, and be able to provide expenses to and from the field of service. The Foreign Mission Board will provide housing, utilities, and transportation on the field.

The Special Project Program entails persons of special skills to serve one year. The Foreign Mission Board will pay travel to and from the field, housing, and utilities. For more detailed information on such special skills as nurses, technicians, printers, teachers, etc., write to Volunteer or Special Project Program, Foreign Mission Board, SBC, Box 6597, Richmond, Virginia, 23230

2. *Southern Baptist Home Mission Board:*
Home Mission Board Opportunities

The Christian Service Corps is a program sponsored by the Special Missions Ministries Department of the Home Mission Board. It is a program whereby lay volunteers serve in mission opportunities and needs throughout the United States.

Short-term Program

There is a short-term program where people are needed from two weeks to one year. The program calls for adults who qualify to serve without pay, to provide their own transportation to and from the field, to provide their own room and board when arrangements cannot be made to stay in a home on the field, and any other expense. The Home Mission Board assumes *no financial obligations*.

Some opportunities include: Vacation Bible Schools, surveys, office work, music, construction work, leadership in teaching ministries, and other areas.

Long-term Program

This program is much like the short-term program in that the lay volunteer assumes total financial responsibility. The volunteer moves to the mission field, assumes an occupation he is qualified for, and during his leisure and on week-ends helps the regular appointed missionary. He may remain on the field the rest of his life as a volunteer.

Opportunities for service are available in the Northeast, North Central, Midwest, Far West, and Pacific Northwest. For more information contact:

Christian Service Corps
Special Missions Ministries
Home Mission Board
1350 Spring Street, N.W.
Atlanta, Georgia 30309

3. *Governmental Programs:*

For a more detailed description of the following suggestions, write for the

AOA Fact Sheet
DHEW Publication
No. (OHD) 76-20233
National Clearinghouse on Aging
Washington, D.C. 20201

(1) Where to look for jobs:

state employment service office

Professional or trade associations
labor union employment services
churches
YWCA/YMCA vocational services
nonprofit volunteer employment agencies
private temporary employment agencies
(2) Programs to consider:
A. Programs Under Action
(a) *Foster Grandparent Program*—for persons sixty years of age or older, in good health, who can work four hours a day, five days a week, giving two hours each day to each of two children entrusted in their care. A stipend is offered for this service. For more information write to:

> Foster Grandparents
> Program/Action
> 806 Connecticut Avenue, N.W.
> Washington, D.C. 20525

(b) *Retired Senior Volunteer Program* (RSVP)—This RSVP program is for persons sixty and over who are willing to donate their lives to programs such as daycare, Boy and Girl Scout offices, courts, schools, libraries, nursing homes, etc. Reimbursement for expenses can be arranged. Contact:

> RSVP Program/Action
> Washington, D.C. 20525

(c) *SCORE* (Service Corp's of Retired Executives)—A program of volunteer retired executives who donate their expertise in management techniques to small businesses and community organizations. Write:

SCORE/Action
Washington, D.C. 20525

(d) *VISTA* (Volunteers in Service to America)—This program is for persons of all ages who display specific skills who can give one year to serve with migrant families on Indian reservations, in mentally handicapped institutions, etc. Contact:

Vista/Action
Washington, D.C. 20525

(e) *Peace Corps*—Is a program where persons serve a minimum of two years in overseas service. Such skilled areas needed include teaching (math, science), teacher training, vocational trades, etc. Write:

Peace Corps/Action
806 Connecticut Avenue, N.W.
Washington, D.C. 20525

(f) *ACTION Cooperative* Volunteers—A program for all ages to contribute one year in public and private nonprofit agencies in all levels of education, health, probation, etc. Write to:

Action Cooperative Volunteers
806 Connecticut Avenue, N.W.
Washington, D.C. 20525

B. U.S. Department of Labor Programs—Programs available to older Americans for work and training. *These programs may not be available in every state,* so write each program for availability.

(a) *Green Thumb*—A background in farming is essential as workers are employed part-time in conservation, beautification, and community projects. For information write:

> Green Thumb, Inc.
> 1012 14th Street, N.W.
> Washington, D.C. 20005

(b) *Senior Aides*—A wide variety of jobs are in this program. Contact:

> National Council of Senior Citizens
> 1511 K Street, N.W.
> Washington, D.C. 20005

(c) *Senior Community Service Project*—This program offers a variety of part-time work in community services such as Social Security, public housing, hospitals, schools, etc. For further detailed information, write to:

> National Council on Aging
> 1828 L. Street, N.W.
> Washington, D.C. 20036

(d) *Senior Community Service Employment Program*—This program is sponsored by the National Retired Teachers Association and the American Association of Retired Persons. It aids in part-time work for semiskilled and unskilled job opportunities. Detailed descriptions can be obtained by writing:

> NRTA/AARP
> 1909 K Street, N.W.
> Washington, D.C. 20006

(e) *Senior Community Service Employment Program*—A program administered by the Forest Service involves work in conservation—beautification projects.

Contact:

>U.S. Department of Agriculture
>Forest Service
>Washington, D.C. 20250

C. Other Government Programs

(a) *Teacher Corps*—A program designed to help disadvantaged children in poverty areas. Write for more information to:

>Teacher Corps
>Office of Education
>Washington, D.C. 20202

(b) *Adult Basic Education*—Contact the director of adult education in your state department of education. These opportunities of helping people over sixteen years of age complete their education can be discovered.

(c) *Census Surveys*—A program where older persons may serve as part-time interviewers is available by contacting a Census Bureau Data Collection Center nearest you.

(d) *Veterans Hospital Volunteers*—A program of service such as letter writing, reading to patients, feeding patients, working in admissions, etc. is available by contacting the chief of volunteer service at the nearest VA hospital.

(e) *Federal Job Information Centers*—Through contacting the offices of the U.S. Civil Service Commission, job opportunities for older Americans can be discovered.

For further information on work and Social Security, contact a local Social Security Office.

IV. Ideas for Organization

Idea #144 Ways to Organize

Most senior adult weekday programs are organized in a structural form. The group has a name, officers, and a regular time of meeting. One organizational structure follows this pattern:

Name: Triple L Club
Meeting: Every Thursday
Officers: President
       Vice-President
       Secretary
       Group Captains: Each captain has a list of ten names, addresses, and telephone numbers of members. They are responsible for contacting their list for announcements or for a prayer chain.

There are some senior adult weekday groups that have no structured organization and these work well in most cases. Many of these have a name, but no officers. They do have a person who is the leader of the group and plans and coordinates the activities with the group. This person might be a senior adult or of another age group. Usually such a leader is a church staff member. This person, whether staff or a member needs to have a genuine love for, and understanding of, senior adults.

The recreation staff/committee of a church may have the responsibility of providing opportunities for senior adult weekday programs. If so, it is strongly urged that they promote this function of the recreation program through the existing organizations of the church. In most cases, these activities will be promoted through the Sunday School since it is the largest organization in the church. If the recreation ministry is the sponsoring organization, a representative from the senior adult group should be a member of the recreation staff/committee. This person will be responsible for seeing that money is budgeted in the recreation budget for this weekday ministry, reporting to the recreation staff/committee the plans and events of the senior adult weekday ministry, and ensuring that a balanced program of recreation and ministry be projected for all senior adults in the church.

Whatever the organizational structure might be, it is important that a balanced program of activities which meet the needs and interests of senior adults be established.

Idea #145 Names for Weekday Clubs

Many senior adult groups go by the name, Baptist Senior Adults, others choose a novel name for their group. Here are some examples:

Triple L Club (L.L.L.)—Live Long and Like It

JOY—Just Older Youth

XYZ—Xtra Years of Zest

WOO—Wise Old Owls
OASIS—Older Americans Sharing in Service
SAF—Senior Adult Fellowship
ADY—Ain't Done Yet or Ain't Dead Yet
BALL—Be Active—Live Longer
Keenagers
Eat and Travel Club
Ageless Wonders
SAFO—Senior Adult Fellowship Organization
Actkeens
Heritage
TNT—Twix and Tween
K.I.T.—Keep in Touch
Live embers
Jolly Elders
Young at Heart
Going Like Sixty
Best Agers Club
The Diamond Set
Golden Agers Club
Get Together Club
The Old Guard and Gardenias
Merrymakers
Never Too Old Club
Top Agers Club
Evergreen Club
Second Mile Club
Sunshine Club
Sunbeams

Jewel Club
Golden Harvest
Retired Live Wires
Pioneer Club
The Fossils
Metallic Club (Silver in their hair, gold in their teeth
    and lead in their feet)
Old Cronies
Retirees

Some of these names are humorous, and others more serious. A good idea is to have the group submit and vote on the name for the group. If no name is used, call them Baptist Senior Adults.

Idea #146 A Balanced Program

Too often, weekday clubs will overemphasize one area and that is usually travel. Most senior adults love a short trip or even long excursions. This is a great part of the weekday program ideas, but there should be a well-balanced program for this age group. Some areas to consider:

Worship: Senior adults need the experiences offered through formal and informal worship settings. They not only need these experiences, but need to be involved in the worship process as leaders. These can be accomplished through drama, music, retreats, camping, and other ways. Whatever the methods, senior adults need experiences in worship.

Fellowship: The need for fellowship among other senior

adults as well as with other age groups is needed for senior adults. There are periods of loneliness, especially when one loses a mate, a job, or moves into a new community. Weekday programs provide opportunities for fellowship (*koinonia*) with fellow Christians who have similar needs.

Continued Growth Through Discovering and Acquiring New Knowledge: Through in-depth Bible study, continuing education (skill classes, crafts, college courses, etc.), opportunities to instruct, trips, and the like will be a good source of strength for the senior adult to keep abreast in acquiring new knowledge.

Ministry and Service Activities: Senior adults need to continue to serve the church and community. With their enormous amount of talent and experience, the church should capitalize on this vast wealth of resource. All the leisure time these people have can be put to constructive and purposeful usefulness.

Leisure or Recreational Activities: Even though a major part of a weekday club organization is found in the area of recreational activities, a word on recreation is still needed. Recreation in the church encompasses the following program areas: Arts, crafts, hobbies, camping, drama, recreational music, retreats, social recreation (parties, banquets, fellowships), sports and games, and trips and tours. Some of these have been discussed in more detail in other chapters of the book. But, recreation is a vital part of the weekday club program. However, it too needs to be a balanced program within itself.

Physical Fitness: The physically fit senior adult leads a happier and more active life. This is one area which should be emphasized in the balanced program. Also included in this is nutrition.

Other areas might be listed. Whatever they might be, the total program of the senior adult weekday program should have a healthy balance. One way to discover what the senior adult is interested in can be done by reading the next Idea (# 147).

Idea # 147 Senior Adult Interest Survey

A survey such as this is to help discover the interests of the group, and to help discover potential leadership from the senior adult group. The senior adult leader should first survey the community to discover the resources available for the senior adult as well as to discover places of interest for the senior adult to attend.

In taking the interest survey, it is good to take it on a Sunday morning during a brief period of the Bible study hour. Hand out the survey, explain what the purpose is, give an explanation for each activity listed in the survey, be available for any questions, and take up the surveys as soon as the people complete them. The survey does not have to be too involved. Raymond A. Kader, in his book *Senior Adult Utilization and Ministry Handbook*, has excellent sample surveys and procedures. There is one in the following paragraph.

After the survey is completed by the senior adults,

collect them and compile them. The activities the group shows the most interest in will help in planning the calendar for the senior adults. Here is a sample survey:

Senior Adult Interest Survey

Name: _____

Address: _____

City: _____ State: _____ ZIP_____

Check the appropriate space. Please do not check every opportunity, but only a few in each section which you most want to do. If you can provide leadership, please check the appropriate space. Feel free to make suggestions.

MINISTRY AND SERVICE IDEAS	I would like to do this	I can provide leadership
Telephone reassurance program	_____	_____
Inventory the church	_____	_____
Make posters	_____	_____
Answering service	_____	_____
Eat with a shut-in weekly	_____	_____
Lord's house committee	_____	_____
Handyman program	_____	_____
Office helper		
Church	_____	_____
Associational office	_____	_____
Other_____	_____	_____
_____	_____	_____

WEEKDAY PROGRAM IDEAS	I would like to do this	I can provide Leadership
Social Security	_____	_____
Medicare	_____	_____
Making a will	_____	_____
Income tax preparation	_____	_____
Study world religions	_____	_____
How to witness to senior adults	_____	_____
Game day	_____	_____
Tournaments (checkers, chess, etc.)	_____	_____
Other_____	_____	_____

ARTS, CRAFTS, HOBBIES		
Ceramics	_____	_____
Weaving	_____	_____
Painting (watercolor)	_____	_____
Macrame	_____	_____
Decoupage	_____	_____
Bread dough art	_____	_____
Christmas crafts	_____	_____
Candlemaking	_____	_____
Leathercraft	_____	_____
Quilting	_____	_____
Quilling	_____	_____
Woodwork	_____	_____
Other_____	_____	_____

DRAMA
Choral speaking   _____   _____
Puppetry   _____   _____
Pantomime   _____   _____
Produce a play   _____   _____
Other_____   _____   _____

MUSIC
Senior Adult Choir   _____   _____
Kazoo Band   _____   _____
Handbells   _____   _____
Fun singing   _____   _____
Other_____   _____   _____

SOCIAL RECREATION
Parties   _____   _____
Banquets   _____   _____
Teas   _____   _____
Receptions   _____   _____
Picnics   _____   _____
Other_____   _____   _____

SPORT ACTIVITIES
Horseshoes   _____   _____
Shuffleboard   _____   _____
Fishing   _____   _____
Golf   __ _   _____
Bowling   _____   _____
Bicycling (two or three
    wheeler)   _____   _____
Other_____   _____   _____

PHYSICAL FITNESS CLASS	_____	_____
CAMPING AND RETREATS		
Overnight camping	_____	_____
Family campouts	_____	_____
Day camping	_____	_____
Retreat	_____	_____
Other_____	_____	_____
TRIPS, EXCURSIONS,		
TOURS		
Christmas shopping trip	_____	_____
Go to the fair	_____	_____
Trip to Williamsburg, Virginia	_____	_____
Trip to Hawaii	_____	_____
Trip to an athletic event	_____	_____
Attend a concert	_____	_____
See the autumn leaves	_____	_____
Ridgecrest Chautauqua or Jubilee	_____	_____
Glorieta Chautauqua	_____	_____
Other_____	_____	_____
_____	_____	_____
_____	_____	_____

This is a sample survey. For other ideas of surveys, check Kader's book, or order Talent Survey from Baptist Book Store. A survey might be taken every year or even seasonally. Always offer a different variety in each survey. Sometimes, ask if the group would like to make a return trip or have a repeat feature.

Your survey will depend much upon how often you meet with the group. This will help determine your schedule. Some groups meet weekly, twice a month, or once a month. Your group should decide the number of times they will meet. This will determine your survey length and what to include. Whatever, give the senior adults an opportunity to express their interests.

Idea #148 *Crisis Directory*

With the small print of telephone directories making it difficult for senior adults to locate numbers, prepare a directory for them with large type which includes telephone numbers of various services offered by the community and the church. It is a quick referral for the senior adult, especially in time of crisis. Included in this directory:

  1. *Emergency Services:* Numbers for:
     Police
     Ambulance service
     Poison Control Center
     Contact Standby telephone (twenty-four hour
         listening service)
     Information/referral service
     Government assistance
  2. *Hospital and Nursing Care*
     Nursing homes
     Licensed Practical Nurses Association
     Nurses professional organization
     Special problems

Baptist retirement homes
3. *Personal Problems*
   Alcoholics Anonymous
   Pastoral needs
      Church telephone number
      Pastor's home
   Other Church staff
   Chairman of deacons
   Benevolent committee chairman
4. *Good Grief*
   In case of death, follow this suggested outline:
      (1.) Whom to call first
         Physician to certify death
         Funeral director
         Pastor
         Family and friends
         Family lawyer
      (2.) Decisions to be made
         Date, time, and place of service
         —Date and time should be scheduled to allow friends and relatives time for travel
         —Church members are encouraged to hold services at the church in order to employ all the resources of the faith to meet the grief needs.
         —A meal for family and friends, following the service and burial, is often a meaningful experience. Groups in the church are available for the home or the church.

(3). Visitation hours
    When guests will be received for more than
    one day or when there are limitations on
    the strength and endurance of the family,
    limited and announced hours for visiting are
    suggested.
(4). Casket and vault selection
    Funeral expense
(5.) Burial or cremation
(6.) Clothing for the deceased
(7.) Flowers and/or memorial fund
(8.) Selection of pallbearers
(9.) Watch over house for family while they are
    at the funeral home.
(10.) Usual services from a funeral director
    Newspaper notices
    Embalming and preparation
    Use of funeral home and staff
    Use of motor vehicles
    Some help with Social Security application,
        insurance forms, veteran forms, and other
        legal procedures
    Securing certified copies of death certificate
    Assist in selection of cemetery plot if ar-
        rangements have not been made.
(11.) Telephone numbers of funeral homes
5. *Mental Health*
    For strictly emotional problems call
    Other senior citizens problems call

6. *Education Opportunities*
   Colleges (some state-supported institutions will offer additional or continual education for senior citizens at a nominal cost, and in some cases without charge)
   Senior Citizens Membership Organizations
      Church sponsored
      American Association of Retired Persons
      National Council of Senior Citizens
      National Council on Aging
      Other organizations which may be local
7. *Special Needs*
   Meals-on-wheels
   Consumer information
      Federal, state, local
   Social Security
   Medicare
   Medicaid
   Supplement Security Income
8. *Financial and Legal Problems*
   Consumer credit counseling
   Better Business Bureau
   Legal Aid Society
9. *Volunteer Opportunities*
   Your church
   Your senior adult group
   R.S.V.P. (Retired Senior Volunteer Program)
   Home Mission Board
   Foreign Mission Board

This outline of materials was adapted from a very excellent and attractive brochure given to members of the Senior Achievers of Elfinwild United Presbyterian Church, Glenshaw, Pennsylvania. It contained not only telephone numbers of the above services, but explained what these services offered. It appears to be an excellent idea for churches to follow in providing this type of information for its senior adults. Adapt this idea for your senior adults.

Idea #149 Senior Adult Newsletter

A monthly newsletter especially aimed at senior adults and their needs can be an added plus to a senior adult weekday ministry. This means of communication can be the main piece to publicize programs, bits of news, and other items.

To begin, have a contest to name the newsletter. Many senior adult clubs give their name to the newsletter, but a contest might prove fun in naming the paper. Have a staff of reporters who will contribute to the newsletter or who are responsible for securing writers for the newsletter. This will give senior adults the opportunity to publish creative stories, poems, or recipes. Have a page for birthdays, a section for recipes (especially for senior adults which will provide nourishment), a want ad or for sale section, a calendar of events for the group, church news pertinent to the senior adult, and any other items you might think up.

Idea #150 Using Existing Organizations in the Church

Someone might ask what your church is doing for senior adults or if you have a senior adult ministry. Your answer should be, "Yes." If you have a Sunday School class for this age group, you have a senior adult ministry.

One of the primary needs of senior adults is spiritual growth. The church has program organizations to help meet these spiritual needs. A senior adult needs worship. A time should be set aside for individual worship and corporate worship with fellow Christians of all ages. Therefore, the church offers this part of spiritual development for the senior adult. But, the senior adult also should be a part in creating that worship service. He can serve in many ways to enhance the spirit of worship. Through serving as an usher, participating in the choir, taking up the offering, leading in prayer, reading the Scriptures, leading the music, praying for the pastor, all of these are ways worship can be a vehicle of service for the senior adult.

Bible study is a very important part of the life of a senior adult. Someone stated that the reason senior adults study the Bible so fervently is that they are cramming for final exams. Whatever the reason, good, in-depth Bible study is a must for senior adults. The Sunday School provides for this ministry with excellent materials available in large print designed especially for the senior adult. Other helps for the senior adult are available in large print editions: *Open Windows*, large print Bibles, and various religious books are available at the Baptist Book

Store. A 1977-78 Sunday School emphasis is "Think Senior Adults." A planning guide can be obtained from the Sunday School Department, Sunday School Board, Nashville, Tennessee, 37234.

Church Training offers the senior adult continued development in Christian theology, Baptist doctrine, Christian ethics, Christian history, church polity, and organization. Excellent materials for the senior adult are developed through the Church Training Department of The Sunday School Board. Senior adults need to continually grow and develop as leaders in the church.

Other organizations in the church offer the senior adult opportunities for study in missions. The Woman's Missionary Union and the Baptist Brotherhood provide materials for mission study and mission involvement for the senior adult. The music ministry gives opportunity for musical expression for the senior adult as a leader of choirs or as a participant singing in one of the choirs. There is ample opportunity for the senior adult to be involved in a complete ministry through these organizations, but in many cases, more is desired.

Therefore, other opportunities for fellowship and service can be available through a senior adult weekday ministry. Most of this book deals with ideas for this type of activity. However, let us stress once again, that whenever possible the activities suggested should be channeled through one of these existing organizations—Sunday School, Church Training, the music ministry, or the mission organizations.

Another factor in senior adult ministry which the church needs to consider is the provision a church offers senior adults in the way of facilities and other services. Consider these areas in your church for senior adults:

—temperature and ventilation
—non-glare lighting
—skid-proof floors
—adequate sound system and hearing aids
—printed materials easy on the eyes
—seating that is comfortable and where it is easy to rise
—doorways and ramps for wheelchairs
—railings on stairs; elevators where needed
—restroom accessible with stalls with handrails
—education space close to worship area
—counseling service
—legal services
—telephone reassurance
—meal service
—transportation
—library service
—medical service

The church has programs already in action for and with senior adults. Hopefully, this chapter will help you in expanding or improving your ministry.

The National Association of Baptist Senior Adults

There is a national organization for retired Baptists that has much to offer the individual senior adult. The National Association of Baptist Senior Adults is an organi-

zation for senior adults and their leaders who enjoy be-
longing to a fellowship of people with common interests
and concerns. Membership is open to Baptists 60 years
of age or older. There is no cost to belong.

To join this association a person should write to:

>Baptist Senior Adults
>Family Ministry Department
>The Sunday School Board
>127 Ninth Avenue, North
>Nashville, Tennessee 37234

For $1.00, the member can receive an attractive lapel
pin. Other benefits received by applying for membership
are a membership card, a transfer decal suitable for a car,
window, door, or other use, news of significant events
such as the Chautauquas, Jubilees, trips, etc., and other
important facts.

Mature Living magazine is a Southern Baptist monthly
publication which is designed primarily for senior adults.
An individual subscription or church subscription can be
purchased by ordering the magazine from the

>Materials Services Department
>127 Ninth Avenue, North
>Nashville, Tennessee 37234.

Conclusion:

Hopefully, this volume has stimulated you to do something with those persons in your church labeled as senior
adults. They are just people, but extraordinary in the
talents they possess. They wait to serve; they wait to
be led; they wait to be given the opportunity to fill leisure
hours; they wait on you.